The BOOK of HOPE

Never failing words of encouragement from the Scriptures

Dave Bailey Sr.

Gazelle
PRESS
Mobile, Alabama

The Book of Hope
by Dave Bailey, Sr.
Copyright ©2013 Dave Bailey, Sr.

ISBN 978-1-58169-487-1
For Worldwide Distribution
Printed in the U.S.A.

Gazelle Press
P.O. Box 191540 • Mobile, AL 36619
800-367-8203

Foreword

Any time Reverend Dave Bailey speaks or writes, it is worth our attention, and this may be especially true when he writes about hope. He named his famous rescue mission "Ranch Hope," and has lived its motto: "An Expectation of Success."

These mediations are Bible-based, and they are laced with vivid human stories. Dave's insights into the Bible texts are often blended with his personal life experiences out of the years of ministry at Ranch Hope. He also manages to find positive quotations about hope from a great variety of sources, including some very unlikely ones, proving that even the godless recognize the value and power of hope.

Many in our time have fallen into the habit of trying to squelch hope, always ready to tell you "Don't get your hopes up!" But this book lights up the Bible's roadmap to understanding the difference between hoping and just wishing. It will help you put that pessimistic advice behind you and look forward and upward with the same "expectation of success" that has energized this man in his remarkable achievements.

It's a good book for "dipping," when you don't have much time for reading. Open to any page and spend some time there. It will brighten your day.

—*Donald Barnhouse*

Acknowledgments

It is important to thank three key people who helped me complete this work. First, my wife who encouraged me when I ran out of inspiration and perspiration. She also read some of the material and offered a much needed critique. Elaine Dunner, who is the head of the Development office at Ranch Hope, gave me valuable assistance in transferring my written word to the computer and preparing the text for the publisher. Stephanie Roagers, my assistant at Ranch Hope, took dictation, retyped nearly every chapter, kept accurate records of each one, helped with all the necessary corrections, and prepared the final draft that was mailed to the publisher. I needed a great deal of hope to keep my eye on the finish line, and these three ladies helped me across it.

Finally I want to acknowledge my ultimate source of hope who called me to the ministry of the Gospel nearly sixty years ago. As you read this book, you will understand why the Lord Jesus is my Rock and my Redeemer and gives me hope every day.

—*Dave Bailey, Sr.*

Ideas on How To Use This Book

Before you begin: Sit quietly for 30 seconds or so to settle your spirit. Take a few deep breaths and get comfortable.

Read: Open your Bible and read the portion of scripture. after you read, pause to think about the passage. What comes to mind? What captured your attention?

Quoted verse: The quoted verse relates to the central point of the meditation. Read it slowly and think about its meaning.

Story: These stories are written to give you hope. How does this chapter help?

Prayer: To end your quiet time, pray. You may want to pray for people or situations that come to mind during your reflection.

Introduction

This book is a look at every verse in the Bible that mentions the word "hope." Hope has always been a favorite word in my vocabulary since my early ministry. We chose the name Ranch Hope for our ministry to youth. It has been a life dream to write a book centered on the word hope as it appears in the Bible.

I have always defined hope as "an expectation of success." Ranch Hope is a ministry that expects success in all that we strive to do. We are continually motivated by the values taught to us by our Lord and Savior, Jesus Christ. By mentoring His way to the children entrusted to us, we believe every child can learn; we believe every child can grow; we believe every child can succeed.

This book has taken nearly four years to write. Each time I thought it was complete, another verse with hope would be found. I used three different translations of the Bible and found hope may appear in one and not another. When you compare a verse in this book with your Bible, there may be a different translation for the word hope. But the root meaning of the word is the same. It is also a certainty that I have missed a verse, and you will find one I did not include. Let me know and I'll include it in the next book.

This book grew out of our experiences in helping young people become disciples of hope. We hope that as you read this collection of scripture you will discover what God-inspired people teach us today about hope. Enjoy the journey!

Don't **EVER** GIVE UP!

~ 1 ~

Ruth 1:12 (NIV) – *"Naomi said, '. . . Even if I thought there was still hope for me.'"*

It is difficult to believe as we begin our study about hope that Ruth is the first book of the Bible to use the word. The word hope is not found in the Pentateuch, Joshua, or Judges. The book of Ruth seems an odd place to find hope in the very first chapter.

Naomi had no reason to hope. Her husband was dead, as were her two sons. She was in a foreign nation and had two daughters-in-law, both of another faith. After her personal tragedies, she wanted to send both of them back to Moab and settle down to a life of bitterness. Little wonder, then, that she had no "expectation of success." But her life was to be dramatically changed by her daughter-in-law, Ruth. Ruth in Hebrew means "beauty," and this is exactly what she was to bring into the life of this widow. Naomi was to find hope in a person God directed into her life. One who is remembered for that oft-quoted love phrase, "Where you go I will go, and where you stay I will stay. Your people will be my people and your God my God." Hope often does come in the form of a person.

Over the years at the Ranch there have been a multitude of people helping us bring hope to troubled youth. Even before the first boy arrived, the Lord directed a printer into my life that proved to be "hopeful." He was a godly man and headed a successful printing business in a community not far from where we would begin the ministry to young people. However, what made him especially remarkable was not his business ability, but rather his ability to overcome adversity. I discovered in my first visit to his printing plant that he was paralyzed from the waist down. This did not deter his activity in the community. He was involved in a service club, scouting, and especially his church. What an inspirational person! What a testimony of hope. After hearing about our dream of building a ranch for troubled boys, he directed one of his staff to help us with a logo, letterheads, and the important first brochure to help publicize the infant ministry. Until his death, John Cowan continued to be interested in the Ranch and never charged for any of the materials his company printed for us.

A popular song has lyrics, which say that people who need people are the luckiest people on earth. Naomi needed Ruth, and Ruth needed Boaz. There is a great deal of hope in the book of Ruth. Remember, Ruth had three strikes against her—in a time when children were considered a blessing from God, she was childless; when wives were dependent on husbands, she was a widow; and where community was important, she was an outsider. So read the entire book and think of people who have been a part of your life—especially those who brought hope where it seemed hopeless. Today may be one of those times when it is difficult to have any hope. Remember Naomi, that Old Testament inspiration, and also John Cowan, and you too can be hope-filled today.

> "Love recognizes no barriers. It jumps hurdles, leaps fences, penetrates walls to arrive at its destination full of hope." *—Maya Angelou*

~ 2 ~

Ezra 10:2 (NIV) – *"But in spite of this, there is still hope for Israel."*

The Jews had returned from a period of captivity. However, there were a number of problems for this remnant. Ezra was a great religious leader at this time, and he had been going through a time of prayer and fasting for his own sins and the sins of his people. It had been quite an emotional experience as people openly wept about their relationship to God and confessed areas of weakness and evil. God used Ezra to rebuild the temple, once destroyed by enemies of the Jews, but the people quickly regressed into breaking God's laws. No longer were they living lives separated from the world but rather were deeply involved in many heathen practices. This seems incredible until we remember how quickly people seem to forget God's blessing. Thus it was a time of hopelessness, when it should have been a time of victory after the horrible years in captivity. Interestingly enough, Ezra does have a word of hope for the people: "In spite of this, there is hope for Israel." Hope often does come as a result of seeing spiritual failure in our own life. Hope can be a spiritual result of praying, fasting, and confessing our sins.

A number of years ago a young man arrived at the Ranch who had been a constant problem in his home and at school. However, he was very likeable and won his way into our hearts. Because of his "cuteness" and personality, our staff found it difficult to believe he was as troubled as others said he was. In a short time, however, this was to change. A pattern of acting out and not admitting to it was soon discovered. Although the boy was with us for an extended period of time, he was never reached and was returned home rather than graduating from the program. It was little wonder, then, that a few short years later we received word that he was in prison. The pattern continued of not being responsible for his actions.

But this is not the end of the story. You can imagine, therefore, how delighted we were when we were told later that he had gone through a spiritual transformation in prison. Hope began for him as he prayed and confessed the evils in his own life. In spite of all that had happened in his life, "there was hope in Israel." Our Lord has a way of taking hopeless lives and making them hopeful. Like the prodigal in Jesus' parable, the young man was "far from the father," incarcerated and alone. In spite of this there was hope for him. The message of salvation he had heard at the Ranch finally took root . Maybe today you know a person who has rejected the gospel. Don't give up on a child, grandchild, or other family members or friends. Hope has never given up!

Best poem in the world:
I was shocked, confused, bewildered
as I entered Heaven's door,
Not by the beauty of it all,
by the lights or its decor.

But it was the folks in Heaven
who made me sputter and gasp—
the thieves, the liars, the sinners,
the alcoholics, the trash.
There stood the kid from seventh grade
who swiped my lunch money twice.
Next to him was my old neighbor
who never said anything nice.

Herb, who I always thought
was rotting away in hell,
was sitting pretty on cloud nine,
looking incredibly well.

I nudged Jesus, "What's the deal?
I would love to hear Your take.
How'd all these sinners get up here?
God must've made a mistake.

"And why's everyone so quiet,
so somber? Give me a clue."
"Hush, child," said He, "They're all in shock.
No one thought they'd see you."

"Learn from yesterday, live for today, hope for tomorrow." –*Albert Einstein*

~ 3 ~

Job 4:6 (NIV) – *"Should not piety be your confidence
and your blameless ways your hope?"*

Job has been visited by his friends. You will remember that
these friends have already determined why Job is going through
his suffering. In spite of all his outward acts of holiness and
goodness, secretly he has been involved with many sins.
Reminds me of the old quotation, "With friends like this, who
needs enemies?" We must at least give the friends credit for
taking time to try and assist Job. In most references to this Bible
story, the friends are criticized, but I have only occasionally

heard them praised for at least visiting. Unfortunately they arrive at the wrong conclusions and only add to Job's problems. They are most sarcastic in telling him that his hope should be based on his piety and blameless ways. We do not need that type of sarcasm during times of trial. Think of those who were not blameless and pious at one point in their life, yet God used them.

At the Ranch we will periodically meet a young person who is convinced his problems are punishment from God. Because he disobeyed at school or lied to his parents or stole something at the local supermarket, God is getting even. One young person in particular comes to mind. His concept of God and religion almost bordered on the occult or magic. He was constantly trying to make a deal with God. Basically it was nothing more than a youthful attempt at manipulation. One night he ran away and was gone nearly six hours. Without our knowledge he was deep in the woods that border the Ranch and was very fearful. Later when he safely returned, he told of running and praying, running and praying, and promising to never leave again (sound familiar?). "I even told the Lord I would be a Christian forever and confessed all my sins to Him," he blurted out between sobs. "And you know what? The Lord brought me right back on the path to the cottage." In his young mind the deal was completed, and because of his "conversion experience," God had brought him out of the deep, dark woods. It is never easy to help a young person understand that God doesn't work that way. However, some of us even in our adult life continue to think that way.

God does not punish us by sending illness or calamity. Sometimes difficulties are the result of our bad choices. Job's friends do not reflect the kind of God we know through Jesus!

But since it's such a common reaction, maybe we sometimes need to express the feeling. Then we can clear it away and move on to the truth of God's unwavering love and care, the truth of God's desire for good and health and wholeness for each of us. King David asked a question recorded in Psalms 6:2: "How long?" It was really a statement of faith. For while the duration of our struggle may be uncertain, the reality of God's presence is never in doubt. As Psalms 6:4 continues, God's love for us is never in doubt; it is "steadfast."

Our hope is not based upon a God that is manipulated by either good or bad deeds. We can be confident today and have an expectation of success because our hope rests upon a loving God and not our piety or blameless ways.

> "We must accept finite disappointment, but never lose infinite hope." –*Martin Luther King Jr.*

~ 4 ~

Job 5:16 (NIV) – *"So the poor have hope."*

Once again, our verse of Scripture records the words of a friend to Job. This friend (Eliphaz) is explaining to Job that trouble in this world is inevitable. Because of this fact, the friend advises Job to seek God, and then goes on to describe the greatness of God. You can imagine how Job felt at this point. He is a godly man who is going through unbelievable distress, and this friend is giving a lesson in theology; just what we all need during such times. It is during this discourse that our verse for today is found. Eliphaz reminds Job that God is concerned for the poor and they too have hope.

Every generation of man to inhabit the earth has had its poor. Obviously the term is used to denote poverty on a material level. Jesus called upon his followers to find happiness by being "poor in spirit," but most references to the poor have to do with lack of material things. I had no idea how poor people could be until traveling to the inner cities of our state to help troubled children and their troubled families. In my childhood and youth I lived in substandard housing, with an outside "privy" and only cold water in the house, with no bathing facilities and coal stoves, but this was not poverty. Our family never really wanted, as my father and mother worked hard to provide us with all the basic necessities of life. Thus seeing real "poor" people was a shock. But being poor in spirit is a real problem. Note the following story that puts everything in perspective.

The ninety-two-year-old petite, proud lady, who is fully dressed each morning by eight o'clock, with her hair fashionably coiffed and makeup perfectly applied, even though she is legally blind, moved to a nursing home. Her husband of seventy years recently passed away, making the move necessary. Some thought she was impoverished, living on limited income. After many hours of waiting patiently in the lobby of the nursing home, she smiled sweetly when told her room was ready. As she maneuvered her walker to the elevator, the nurse provided a visual description of her tiny room with very limited furnishings.

"I love it."

"Mrs. Jones, you haven't seen the room—just wait," said the nurse.

"That doesn't have anything at all to do with it," she replied. "Happiness is something you decide on ahead of time. Whether

I like my room or not doesn't depend on how the furniture is arranged; it's how I arrange my mind. I already decided to love it. It's a decision I make every morning when I wake up. I can spend the day in bed recounting the difficulty I have with the parts of my body that no longer work, or get out of bed and be thankful for what I have. Each day is a gift, and as long as my eyes open, I'll focus on the new day and all the happy memories I've stored away—just for this time in my life. Old age is like a bank account—you withdraw from what you've put in."

So my advice to you would be to deposit a lot of happiness in the bank account of memories. Thank you for your part in filling my memory bank. I am still depositing.

Today you may know about poverty firsthand, or you may be involved in helping in a ministry that reaches the poor at home or overseas. But remember there is nothing like getting out of our comfort zone and bringing hope, financially or spiritually, to the least of those my brethren.

"Lord, save us all from a hope tree that has lost the faculty of putting out blossoms." *–Mark Twain*

~ 5 ~

Job 6:11 (NIV) – *"What strength do I have, that I should still hope?"*

The thought for today centers in the word strength and its relationship to hope. Job, in his state of depression, uses analogy after analogy reviewing his desperate state. He speaks of his anguish being heavier than the sands of the sea; poisonous arrows have been sent directly from Almighty God. Every imaginable terror stalks him; even food makes him ill. He wants God to kill him, for death seems his only escape and hope. So this question is a natural outgrowth of such thinking. In such a weakened state emotionally, physically, and spiritually, can he find any strength? In fact, he implies that he does not have enough strength to even HOPE. Now that is an unenviable position.

Hope, however, is our greatest ally during such times. We expect to succeed even when all strength seems drained from us. Hope, therefore, is not limited by our strength or lack of it. Years ago in college, I was educated to this fact, not in an academic classroom but on the wrestling team.

Our college decided it was time to have a team represent it in a wrestling competition. There is probably no greater challenge to a sports program, a coach, or the students who volunteer than to start a new team. I was one of those unfortunate few who put on the sweat suit and started working out for the "Green Terrors." To make matters even worse, my credentials and experience with wrestling were suspect. I had never even seen a college wrestling match. After weeks of endless practice, the season started, and very quickly my record soared to no wins, three losses. Dramatic changes had to be made.

Unfortunately, my game plan involved a shortcut. What I needed was strength, not more skill. While reading a periodical on sports, I came across an advertisement. The advertisement promised almost immediate results. It said, "Add muscles, add weight, add strength by taking two tablespoons per day." The order was placed, the bottle arrived, and I began religiously taking my two tablespoons of what appeared to be a cross between Geritol and old motor oil.

However, the desired results did not take place, and I was forced to double the dosage and multiply my physical problems. Hope for wrestling fame was centered in the ingredients of a brown bottle that soon caused my neck to be covered with boils and my eyes filled with sties; so much for strength and hope. So much for my future as a wrestler.

Job and I learned that there were no shortcuts to strength, especially spiritual strength. He later asks, "Do I have any power to help myself?" Of course not, Job; none of us do. Our strength still cometh from the Lord.

> "I tremble for my country when I hear of confidence expressed in me. I know too well my weakness, that our hope is in God." *–Robert E. Lee*

~ 6 ~

Job 6:20 (NIV) – *"When caravans stopped for water, their hopes were dashed."*

Today's verse refers to disappointment that came to wandering caravans. Job is speaking of wandering people who had a need of water. Because of past experiences, they knew that the gorges in the area would have water from the melting ice and snow of winter. You can imagine what it must have been like to travel this great distance fully expecting to find water and then to arrive and find everything dry. The brooks were empty and the caravans were thirsty; as some young people would say, "Disappointment to the max." Job applies this to his friends and relates to God his shame and disappointment with them. Obviously he had hoped for better counsel and sympathy.

Have you ever been disappointed by a friend? I can almost anticipate your reply, "How much time to you have, Dave?" All of us could relate some episode from life that could answer that question. A few years ago, a man came to see me after being released from prison. I found him to be an interesting conversationalist and his life story more than intriguing. He had just served five years for armed robbery and had studied theology and the Bible while incarcerated. Now out of prison, he was anxious to get on with his new life "in Christ." I, too, was anxious to help, and we soon found a position on our staff for this new friend.

In addition to giving him a job, we also took him to a local merchant and bought him a new suit. A new suit for the new man. The first few weeks, the ex-prisoner was all we had hoped he would be. He was an excellent speaker at chapel, a hard worker, and a good example to the boys. However, the roof soon fell in. Problems surfaced that were devastating. Without our knowledge, he had fallen in love with another man's wife, and in a time of weakness, they ran away together. As if this were not enough, matters were further complicated by the fact that, together, they reverted to his old lifestyle, armed robbery. And to think some of those armed robberies were carried out with him wearing that handsome suit we had bought him. Talk about disappointment.

Today, he is back in prison. The woman and her family are reunited. As for me, I am somewhat wiser. Thank God that our hope is not built solely upon people. From time to time some of them will disappoint us. Our thirst is quenched by the Savior who gives us living water. This living water helps us learn to live with hope even when friends disappoint us.

"Just as despair can come to one from other human beings, hope too can be given to one by other human beings." *–Elie Wiesel*

~ 7 ~

Job 7:6 (NIV*)* – *"My days are swifter than a weaver's shuttle, and they come to an end without hope."*

Today's verse is part of a long description of the brevity of life. Job is still in a state of deep depression and wishes he were dead. Devotion seven is not to be read when you are down. It probably is one of the most depressing chapters in the entire Old Testament. He speaks of his weary nights when he can't sleep, his poor physical condition, terrifying dreams and visions. Finally in total desperation, he bitterly accuses God of mistreating him and then lists twenty complaints. You can see why he says, "Life is fast and comes to an end without hope." What makes this even more tragic is that we are dealing with a godly man. In the opening chapter of the book of Job, the reader is told that Job feared God and shunned evil. This is an important point to remember in terms of our own spiritual growth. None of us is immune to events that could lead to depression.

Youth work has enough stress and anxiety associated with it that everyone in our ministry must be careful of "burnout." Burnout is so insidious that you can't always predict when it is taking control of your life. A psychologist many years ago said it is like a bucket of water being filled with stones. One by one the stones are dropped into the bucket, and you are never sure which stone will make the water overflow out of the bucket. So problems come in life, and we are never sure which one will do a negative work in us. We can deal with many stressful situations on a day-by-day basis and cope quite effectively, but who knows which one could lead to depression or burnout.

Oswald Chambers, in his classic *My Utmost For His Highest*, takes an additional look at this condition and calls it spiritual leakage. He refers to the verse, "Behold, as the eyes of servants look unto the hand of their masters . . . so our eyes wait upon the Lord our God"(Psalm 123:2).

This verse is a description of entire reliance upon God. Just as the eyes of the servant are riveted on his master, so our eyes are up unto God, and our knowledge of His countenance is gained (cf. Isaiah 53:1. R.V). Spiritual leakage begins when we cease to lift up our eyes unto Him. The leakage comes not so much through trouble on the outside as in the imagination; when we begin to say: "I expect I have been stretching myself a bit too much, standing on tiptoe and trying to look like God instead of being an ordinary humble person." We have to realize that no effort can be too high.

For instance, you came to a crisis when you made a stand for God and had the witness of the Spirit that all was right, but the weeks have gone by, and the years maybe, and you are slowly coming to the conclusion, "Well, after all, was I not a bit too pretentious? Was I not taking a stand a bit too high?" Your rational friends come and say, "Don't be a fool; we knew when you talked about this spiritual awakening that it was a passing impulse. You can't keep up the strain; God does not expect you to." And you say, "Well, I suppose I was expecting too much." It sounds humble to say it, but it means that reliance on God has

14

gone and reliance on worldly opinion has come in. The danger is lest no longer relying on God you ignore the lifting up of your eyes to Him. Only when God brings you to a sudden halt will you realize how you have been losing out. Whenever there is a leakage, remedy it immediately. Recognize that something has been coming between you and God, and get it readjusted at once.

> "Hope is the thing with feathers that perches in the soul —and sings the tunes without the words—and never stops at all." *–Emily Dickinson*

~ **8** ~

Job 8:13 (NIV) – *"Such is the destiny of all who forget God, so perishes the hope of the godless."*

Remember, Bildad the Shuhite is "consoling" Job. He is calling Job godless. In fact, in the King James translation of the Bible, the word used here is hypocrite. "The hypocrite's hope shall perish; it will be like a spider's web." One wonders if Bildad was aware of the many implications in calling Job a hypocrite. Here are a few of the definitions of a hypocrite taken from the Hebrew: one who acts a false part; one who makes a false profession; a cheat; a deceiver; an imposter; a pretender; one who wants to prosper through misleading people. It should be added at this point that to make matters worse, the closing phrase "shall be cut off" can be translated, "his support shall rot away." So much for the friends who seek to counsel.

Keeping the verse in context as it refers to Job, there is a spiritual truth here. Hope for the godly person cannot be built upon hypocrisy. It will be like a spider web. We've all had experiences with the delicate creation of a spider. Webs can be very attractive but, of course, are death traps for unsuspecting victims. Still we know they're not very strong when confronted by the human body or some other heavy weight. How quickly they are destroyed. A few years ago, we were in desperate straits here at the Ranch. Every attempt was made to solicit funds from our contributors and find some new avenues of fund-raising. In spite of all these efforts, we continued in our slide toward economic failure. It was at this point that we were visited by a "professional fund-raiser." Having worked with many nonprofit organizations, it was his point of view that we needed a special event to reach new sources of revenue and "quick cash." He and I negotiated a contract and, after setting carefully discussed guidelines, we presented a plan to the Ranch Hope Board of Managers. The board was not greatly impressed, but based on our financial conditions decided to give it a try.

Problems started almost immediately. The guidelines we negotiated to protect Ranch Hope's integrity were one by one ignored. When the "campaign" was completed, we had a file of letters and phone calls from disgruntled people. High pressure solicitation over the phone, activity in areas of the state considered off limits (because we already had fund-raising events there), questionable stories told about boys, and many other areas of concern made this experience horrendous. The only encouraging dimension was that we received $15,000.00 that helped us limp through the remainder of the year. You can imagine how discouraged we were to learn later that we were deceived, and Ranch Hope received only a fraction of over $90,000.00 that the "pros" had raised. A lesson was learned through this bitter experience. It was small comfort to remember that "the hypocritical fund-raiser too shall perish." As we confront the hope of the godless, it must be overcome by the H-O-P-E of the godly. The idea of the fund-raiser was a spider web.

> "I hope that I shall possess firmness and virtue enough to maintain what I consider the most enviable of all titles, the characters of an honest man!" *–George Washington*

~ 9 ~

Job 8:13 (NIV) – *"Such is the destiny of all who forget God, so perishes the hope of the godless."*

With a friend like this, Job did not need enemies. Bildad the Shuhite is not very sympathetic to Job's plight and tends to be rather preachy. No one could argue with what he says but rather with his method and timing. Job, as a godly man, would routinely say AMEN to everything written in the eighth devotion. But he was not in the right mood or spiritual condition for such a discourse. But for our study today, we will focus on the truth of Bildad's statement: If we forget God, our hope will perish.

A young man came to Ranch Hope from a neighboring community. He had made good progress and was soon considering leaving the Ranch and returning home. The Ranch had the boy's name engraved on a bracelet and imprinted on a Bible at graduation. I was shocked when this particular boy refused to accept the Bible. "I won't need that, Rev.," he said while leaving with his girlfriend. "I accepted that Jesus stuff while I was here, but I won't need it now." The Bible was carelessly flipped on my desk as he left the office. Almost to the point of tears, I picked up the Bible and placed it on a shelf in my office, then watched the couple drive out the Ranch lane.

About two years later, the young man called and told me of his recent marriage. He was excited about a new job, and they had carefully planned the ceremony and their first steps as husband and wife. Spiritually he had made no progress since he had left the Ranch. A child was born about a year later, and they moved into a recently renovated apartment. Everything seemed to be going well. However, as I returned to my office late one afternoon, I learned that he had been killed in an automobile accident on his way to work at a local plant. The grieving wife asked me to conduct the funeral service.

That week, as I prepared my remarks for the service, I came upon the Bible that the young man had rejected. My thoughts reviewed the experiences in my office as he left the Ranch ready to face the world. His hope was to build upon something less than what God had promised him. However, that day at the funeral, I presented the claims of Christ to those who still had an opportunity to follow a different destiny. It was my hope that friends and family would believe. In the front of the Bible I had written, "This book will keep you from the devil, or the devil will keep you from this book." How true!

Bill had missed the most important message—the "u" in Jesus. Before you were thought of or time had begun, God stuck U in the name of His Son. And each time U pray, you'll see it's true. You can't spell out JesUs and not include U. You're a pretty big part of His wonderful name. For U, He was born; that's why he came. And His great love for U is the reason He died. It even takes U to spell crucified. Isn't it thrilling and splendidly grand He rose from the dead, with U in His plan? When JesUs left earth at His upward ascension, He felt there was one thing He just had to mention. "Go into the world and tell them it's true. That I love them all—just like I love U." Bill failed to realize that he, too, had the right to know Jesus. Now I suggest it all depends on what U will do. He wants us to know Him, but it all starts with U.

> "You are here not merely to make a living. You are here to give the world a finer spirit of hope… you are here to enrich the world." –*St. Thomas Aquinas*

~ 10 ~

Job 11:18 (NIV) – *"You will be secure, because there is hope."*

Zophar is another friend who comes and counsels Job. He and Job have quite a dialogue. Setting aside some of his remarks that prejudge Job, we find some excellent advice. Zophar gives a prescription for security and hope that would be an inspiration to anyone. At this point we see a linkage between being secure and having hope.

It is not easy for a child to leave his home and community and move to a place of strangers. Even if the home and community are threatening, a new place and new people can be even more threatening. Try and put yourself in the position of one such twelve-year-old. He had come from an urban center in New Jersey. When he arrived, he was very frightened and homesick.

After the initial interviews and orientation, he was placed in a cottage with seven other boys. His adjustment was a disaster. A fight broke out between him and another boy. "I'll kill you some night," the older boy shouted. "And I'll kill you," the younger boy cried, making a weak defense. The shouting match caused additional terror in the life of a little boy far from home and feeling very much alone.

The next morning, as the boys were preparing for school, our staff reported that all went well during the night. We had instructed them to keep close watch on the newcomer and provide protection in case the older boy followed through on his threat. When the houseparent was doing his inspection, a discovery was made. The new boy had placed a metal bar under his pillow. The bar was routinely used in weight lifting, but this time our new arrival used it for security against the bully. Thank God he never had to use it. He had hope during that long, restless first night because his security was under the pillow. It is always a delight to take frightened young people and help them find a new security and hope in the Lord Jesus.

All of us can know times of insecurity. (This can happen even in familiar places.) My brothers and sisters served in the military during the Second World War. They often related experiences of insecurity in foreign lands under the duress of combat. But these feelings and emotions can exist even after times of military combat. We combat times of financial, emotional, and other forms of personal insecurity. The Zophar prescription is important—security is based on hope in our eternal God.

> "When we reach the end of our ability to cope—it is in Christ that we need to place our hope." –*Susan Lenzkes*

~ 11 ~

Job 11:20 (NIV) – *"But the eyes of the wicked will fail, and escape will elude them; their hope will become a dying gasp."*

This is the concluding remark in Zophar's first discourse. He had been relating to Job the blessings that come when Job meets the requirements of prayer and righteous living. Then in one brief statement, he passes further judgment on Job and concludes, "The hope of the wicked will be a dying gasp" (paraphrase). Zophar again returns to the popular theology that can be summed up with the words, "You suffer because you sin." Now, obviously, sin can cause suffering, but it is extremely dangerous to equate the two in every circumstance. (Jesus had something to say about this, as recorded in John 9:2 and 3.) However, let us consider the statement, "Their hope will become a dying gasp." It is possible for events in life to bring us to such a point.

Ron was a good-looking young man of thirteen years when he was brought to the Ranch. His mother had died when he was in the second grade, and his father took on the responsibilities of raising Ron along with two other children. The father had a drinking problem and was abusive. Within a short period of time, many problems surfaced that could not be solved by the children or father; social agencies became involved. By the time Ron was in the fifth grade, serious emotional problems caused him to act out in class and eventually be expelled. It was after such a history of problems that he came to Ranch Hope.

Like many youth before him, Ron did not like being at Ranch

Hope. "I hate this place, and I hate all of you," he shouted one day, red with anger, "and I hate my dad for sending me here." Hatred had become a way of life for Ron. The staff looked beyond the hatred and saw a boy hurting. It took nearly three years to pierce the armor of distrust, but little by little hope replaced hate. Ron graduated from the Ranch program, attended a local high school, and was placed with a couple to live until he completed his schooling and could go on "independent living."

The couple Ron moved in with was a preacher and his wife living not far from the Ranch. The wife had taught at the Ranch a few years before this, and it seemed a perfect match. Everything seemed to be working very well in this new home and blessed environment. We were all encouraged when Ron took a job with an insurance company and began to work his way up as a salesman. He soon met a lovely young woman, they were married in the pastor's church, and within two years had their first child. On the surface everything seemed to be going well.

Still, the years of abuse and hopelessness had taken their toll. In spite of many outward appearances of change, inwardly Ron was still an emotional wreck. Late one night he drove his car into a truck, head-on at a high rate of speed, and was killed instantly. To this day we don't know if it was accidental or intentional.

When the news arrived at my home, I was grieved beyond belief. Those early events of Ron's life raced through my mind. My only hope was that he found peace in the presence of our Lord. It underlined for me again that in our Christian walk we must do all we can to overcome hopelessness before it can consume a young person. The dying gasp referred to by Zophar can be written about many tragic lives. Today may each of us recommit ourselves to the "Rons" in our lives and bring them hope—an expectation of success instead of tragedy.

"If I fail, I try again, and again, and again. If YOU fail, are you going to try again . . . If you can't get a miracle, become one." *–Nick Vujicic, Life Without Limits*

~ 12 ~

Job 14:7 (NIV) – *"At least there is hope for a tree: If it is cut down, it will sprout again, and its new shoots will not fail."*

In today's study we look at a verse of Scripture dealing with immortality. Job is reasoning about life and death. In the context of this chapter the Bible does not offer us much hope beyond our earthly existence. Thank God as a Christian we have additional information and live on this side of Jesus' resurrection. But today we will just look at this analogy used by Job relating hope to a tree—a tree that has been cut down, yet still gives off new sprouts and shoots.

When my wife Eileen and I moved into our home, I planted some English box shrubs out front. They survived the first winter and within a few years were healthy, thriving plants adding to the beauty of our ranch. When we celebrated our fourteenth anniversary in the home, those plants began to present a problem. Now they had grown too large and were blocking our windows. After continual pleading by my wife, I performed much-needed surgery on those shrubs. They were cut to the ground, and new, smaller plants took their place. However, I was not prepared for what took place next. One year later the shrubs were thriving plants again and quickly taking over the space that they had formerly possessed. A rich root system still existed underground, and that system provided water and nourishment for quick recovery from my surgery. I could now say with Job, "At least there is hope for a tree (shrub): If it is cut down, it will sprout again."

Certainly those of us living in hope of immortality can see the analogy. Though death cuts us down, we will live again. The resurrection of Jesus and His promises of eternal life for all who believe in Him guarantees us our "sprouting power." Certainly if there is hope for a tree to sprout, there is a greater expectation of success for those of us who live and die in Christ.

John Wooden, who led the UCLA men's basketball team to a record ten NCAA national titles, was named the greatest coach of all time by the "Sporting News" in 2009. Greater than Phil Jackson and his eleven NBA championships with the Chicago Bulls and the Los Angeles Lakers. Greater than Casey Stengel, who managed the New York Yankees to ten World Series titles. Greater than football coaching icons Knute Rockne, Bear Bryant, Paul Brown, and Vince Lombardi. Modern-day coaches still study Wooden's "Pyramid of Success" and his Seven-Point Creed, much like the cadets at West Point analyze Grant's siege of Vicksburg. And why not? If you want to be a successful coach, who better to learn from than the greatest coach of all time? As he approached his one hundredth birthday, Coach Wooden was asked to reflect back on his long and storied career. The interviewer asked, "Why have you lived this good, long life?" After pondering the question for a moment, Wooden answered, "I am very much at peace with myself. I'm not afraid of death."

"Faith looks beyond this transient life—with hope for all eternity. Not with some vague and wistful hope, but with trust and certainty." –*D. DeHaan*

~ 13 ~

Job 19:10 (NIV) – *"He tears me down on every side till I am gone; he uproots my hope like a tree."*

Most of us hope to live a life of tranquility. When we are younger we think of a good job, a loving spouse, children, a nice home, and the routine pleasure of family and friends. Job had all this, and then the calamities set in. Is it any wonder he felt hope had been torn up like a tree?

Years ago one of our staff rented a bulldozer for some work on the Ranch. The old farmhouse had to come down to make room for the new administration building. I watched sadly as the old structure came down. It had been our home when we first moved to the Ranch and then converted to an office. It was not much of a structure, but it was full of memories for me and my family. After the ground was all level and the debris was carried away, our staff member turned his attention to improving the grounds around the building. A black walnut tree had dominated the landscape behind the farmhouse. Our first picture for Ranch publicity was taken of me leaning against that tree looking out, "dreaming" over the empty property. When that tree was uprooted by the bulldozer, I nearly burst into tears. In a sense, I knew how Job felt when his hope was uprooted.

Of course, in Job's situation it was far worse than losing an old tree or a dedicated old farm house. Remember, he lost all his children, all his livestock, and all his buildings and property. Everything of value to Job was destroyed. Sometimes as I watched pictures on TV showing the utter devastation of tornadoes—loss of life and limb—I think of Job and what he endured.

Maybe today you are living with or facing circumstances like Job. Trees and dreams do get uprooted. But we must remember they are still only trees. I miss the old farmhouse where we started, but it was just a farmhouse. We have planted other trees; we have built many buildings. Job lost much, but we know at the end of the story that God replaced everything and even gave him a new family. When trees are torn down, plant new ones; when dreams are shattered, dream new dreams. That's what hope is all about.

"Listen deeply to the hope that lies beneath our frustrations, our anger or our depression." –*David Augsburger*

~ 14 ~

Job 14:19 (NIV) – *"As water wears away stones and torrents wash away the soil, so you destroy a person's hope."*

Job's philosophy of man for the here and hereafter, as recorded in today's verse, would be enough to depress the most ardent believer. Notice the analogy of the earthquake, rocks eroding, and soil being washed away, all relating to the hopelessness of man.

However, it is important to remember that Job is still in a state of deep depression at this point. This is not the best time to interview a person and have them quoted for future generations. It is, however, encouraging to each believer to know that our spiritual forbearers could even think such thoughts. Events of life can wear away our faith, wash away our assurance, and destroy our expectation of success.

Believe it or not—Job contains more verses of hope than any book of the Bible except Psalms. I say that because we don't usually associate "hope" with Job the suffering prophet. Today's verse is evidence to why Job doesn't seem very helpful. He is in a very negative mode and actually has written that God "destroys a person's hope." It is not one of those verses you want to put on the refrigerator to bless the family.

Job uses the illustration of water wearing away stones. We have all seen this in a local lake or in the ocean. Years of water flowing over stones will bring change, and if floodwaters come, they wash away soil, often valuable top soil. So for Job today, hope is washed away by a constant erosion of one faith, and God causes it to happen. Keep in mind this is one of the early conversations that Job is having with a friend, Eliphaz, and it is a part of his evolution from a hurting, humiliated man to one that is ultimately restored and healed.

Destruction of hope does not always happen overnight. It can happen like the erosion of soil, a gradual, progressive experience. The young people that come to us at Ranch Hope are often the result of such a process. I have yet to meet a young person who got up one morning and said, "From today on I am going to become a delinquent." It is more subtle than that. For a troubled teen, hope is often eroded experience by experience. A social worker once noted that delinquency can begin nine months before a child is born. Often the child is conceived in a moment of passion by two people who are themselves troubled. The child is then born into a dysfunctional environment. From childhood to the teen years, these negative experiences shape this individual. Is it any wonder the child is troubled? What an opportunity, however, to introduce them to the good news of Jesus.

At our summer camp meeting, Jim Howe conducts "stretching with the Scripture." Each morning he shares the word, then we do exercises (just right for senior citizens). He also starts with a word for the day. One morning he chose "hope." I listened attentively. Jim shared that he almost lost all hope and was angry with God. His brother was very ill and suffered a debilitating disease, still alive but never to be well again. Then Jim began to lose his eyesight. He was a very talented musician and music teacher but had to retire because of his visual limitation. After retirement he was struck down with serious health issues that nearly killed him. His time in the hospital and later rehab lasted nearly one year. As the son of a preacher he had been raised to love the Lord and serve him, and his faith was challenged to the max. Now sitting in a room doing exercises and hearing him use the word hope, I was thankful he had evolved like Job. Jim had also blamed God, but now, though he is legally blind, he is a man of hope. Every day he begins with one expectation of success—his limitations have been turned into expectations.

Maybe you can relate to this passage today. Events have happened, making it difficult for you to be hopeful. Job was convinced God had ruined him and taken away all his prosperity. The continual actions of minor or major calamities take their toll. But Job eventually saw God with his spiritual eyes and was blessed. Take a moment to remember: "My hope is built on nothing less than Jesus."

"Though the towers and temples of this world fall to dust, we can find our hope in God, who alone we trust."
–Joachim Neander

~ 15 ~

Job 17:15 (KJV) – *"And where is now my hope? as for my hope, who shall see it?"*

Questions! Questions! Questions! Job is complaining directly to God. After a long discourse on death and dying, he asks the question of the day: Where is my hope? Who will be able to see my hope? Some have referred to this as the requiem of a dying man. He is convinced that he is in the process of dying, describing every event right to the opening of his grave. This can be a brutal experience for anyone, and especially one who was so close to God.

My wife and I had a similar experience. Our oldest daughter (then just ten years of age), Lee Ann, died. She had been born with birth defects but seemed to be gaining on her various impairments. The events surrounding her death were traumatic. One afternoon I was called at my office and told that she was "choking to death." With the help of my sister, Doris, we rushed her to the hospital (my wife stayed with our infant son). On the way to the hospital, my sister tried mouth to mouth resuscitation on Lee Ann's struggling body. Just blocks from the hospital, my car ran out of gas, and I literally carried Lee Ann the remaining distance. Doctors were able to revive her, but there was serious brain damage. Later that night, she died.

As a result of the entire experience, I began a long journey into a deep depression. My throat seemed to close as a result of my overrelating to Lee Ann's choking episode. For weeks I was practically an emotional vegetable. Like Job there were questions, questions, questions, and no answers. In my mind, I was dying. Miraculously, hope for me came from an unexpected source. A good friend visited regularly and helped me direct my attention to God's source of healing. He would take me on business trips and just provide me comfort and wise counsel. On one trip we stopped for lunch and I was able to eat soup, the first such food I had ingested for days. The healing process had begun.

Naturally I was spending too much time reliving the events of Lee Ann's death. I was not preaching, fulfilling my responsibilities at the Ranch, being a good husband or father to my two living children, and just out of it. I looked like death warmed over, also having lost weight. But then another miracle—my wife, Eileen, put an album on the stereo. It featured the song "O Happy Day." I listened at first, then began to sing: "He taught me how to watch and pray, and live rejoicing every day." Just the sound of my voice singing those words had an impact on me.

The Spirit of God lifted me from my bed of affliction and started a process that gave me hope! Like Job, I cried out, "Where is now my hope?" And at the graveside and in the months that followed, I knew my hope was still Jesus. Maybe you or someone you know has gone through a similar experience. I remind you with assurance that healing will come.

"Even in the midst of suffering there is hope." *–Dusty Miller, POW, World War II*

~ 16 ~

Job 27:8 (KJV) – *"For what is the hope of the hypocrite, though he hath gained?"*

Many scholars believe Job is the oldest book in the Bible. It can easily be considered one of the oldest books in human history. I say this so you have an idea of how long hypocrites have been around. Job is reminding his readers that hypocrites may even derive worldly advantage and approval, but ultimately God will deal with such a person. "When God hath taken away his soul."

All of us have met hypocrites. To the Greeks, hypocrites originally described an actor on the stage, but it later came to mean one who pretended, or lied. We mentioned earlier how they were defined in Jewish literature. Human history and church history are filled with them. It is recorded in English late in the thirteenth century, for a person pretending to believe feelings he doesn't really have. Jesus had a great deal to say about them. All of us must be on guard that we do not join their ranks. There is a little of the hypocrite in all of us.

One afternoon a man came to visit me at the Ranch. He knew of our ministry and wanted to do the same. His great area of concern was the Native American child. He revealed a vision from the Lord for bringing these young people from the reservation and helping them here in the East. Initially his home would be used, and later a property would be purchased to develop a center especially for Native American boys.

The idea seemed plausible. He was an educator by profession and already had two youth living with him. I tried to encourage him and said we would provide all our resources to help him get started. Over the next few months, he visited a number of times and encouraged us that the work was on its way.

Can you believe we discovered he had been stealing from us and had a history of improprieties with legal and church authorities: The tragedy of a hypocrite using us and using others for his own gain.

Jesus, dealing with the same type, asked the question: "What shall it profit a man if he gains the whole world and loses his own soul? Or what shall be gained in exchange for his soul?" We should pray today that our hope can recognize the hypocrite and also prevent us from being one.

> "We hope that, when the insects take over the world, they will remember with gratitude how we took them along on all our picnics." *–Bill Vaughan*

~ 17 ~

Job 31:24 (KJV) – *"If I have made gold my hope..."*

In this chapter of Job, he lists everything of which he is not guilty: deceit, lust, dishonesty, adultery, injustice, inhumanity, covetousness, idolatry, the list goes on. It is interesting that he includes gold, or confidence in gold. Obviously there were many in his time, as there are today, that have built their expectations of success on gold (the dollar, stocks, bonds, property— just substitute any word).

We are bombarded on television about buying gold. It should be a part of our portfolio; claims are made that gold is recession proof. This may all be well and true, but even gold has its limitation. These material possessions do give us some security but not our ultimate source of HOPE.

Before starting the Ranch, I served a church where one of our members was a very wealthy man. He had accumulated great status in the community and was revered by some, despised by others. Although active in the local church and generous in his giving, he was not known as a spiritual leader. Much of his wealth had been attained during the Great Depression at the expense of local farmers. You can imagine the antagonism that existed in the church and community.

Just after I left the church and started to raise funds for Ranch Hope, this man was taken to the hospital for a serious operation. The last time I saw him was in the post-operative room where we prayed and then said our farewells. Later I heard of his death. In discussing his demise, someone asked, "How much did he leave?" A spokesman for the local bank has been reported to say, "He left it all!"

Job knew he, too, would leave it all. You and I know this fact of life. Billy Graham has been quoted saying, "I've never seen a U-Haul on the end of a hearse." Gold is not our hope, nor stocks and bonds. Recessions and depressions come in the financial cycles of any economy. Jesus told us not to lay up treasures that moth and rust could corrupt, because He knew they brought limited hope.

We must be wise stewards (those who look after or manage

something) of material wealth, whatever form that may take—but remember Job lost it all. After all his deprivation, he could say, "I have heard of Thee by the hearing of the ear, but now mine eye seeth Thee." We can build on that testimony today.

"If money is your hope for independence, you will never have it. The real security is a reserve of knowledge, experience, and ability." *–Henry Ford*

~ 18 ~

Job 41:9 (NKJV) – *"Indeed, any hope of overcoming him [the Leviathan] is false; shall one not be overwhelmed at the sight of him?"*

Have you ever seen a Leviathan? Better yet, have you ever even heard of one? For the people of Job's time it was both real and from the realm of myth. It comes up in their discussion of God's omnipotence (all-powerfulness) and Job's impotence. Job has been complaining to God, even challenging God's plan and design for the universe. Believe it or not, Job attempts to be on an equal footing with God, so God begins to review His creation from the very beginning—and reminds Job that he wasn't there. Everything Job knows about the stars, the weather, night and day, the animal kingdom, the birds of the air, good and evil are all second-hand knowledge. So how could Job possibly think he could overcome this dreaded Leviathan?

There are a number of interpretations defining this ancient monster. Earlier, the Lord referred to a behemoth. This was a land creature, possibly an elephant or even a dinosaur, or some other mythical beast. But Leviathan is a beast of the sea, referred to by the ancient Hebrews as a sea monster or sea serpent (probably what we would call today a crocodile). The critical point is that God is asking Job rhetorical questions to which there really is no answer for Job. Job cannot control the Leviathan; he can't hook it or snare it with any line; indeed, any hope of overcoming him is false.

It reminds me of the humorous story about the atheist who is fishing with a friend in Scotland. The fishing buddy knows that the Scot has no belief in God and is an outspoken advocate for unbelief. Suddenly, in the middle of the fishing expedition, the Loch Ness Monster appears next to the boat, and the atheist starts screaming, "Help us, Lord!" The friend is annoyed and reminds the atheist, "You don't believe in God," to which the unbeliever responds, "Well, I didn't believe in the Loch Ness either two minutes ago." So much for unbelief when confronting the monster of life, and for Job the Leviathan is symbolic of all the chaos, evil, and destruction in the world. God wants to remind Job that only He can control and destroy evil. Job must accept this eternal truth.

But there is an even deeper message for Job and for us today. As we read chapter 41 in its entirety, there is a underlying belief on the part of Job that God owes him something for being righteous. It is almost as though Job also believes God owes him restitution for all he has lost. No! No! No! We are not rewarded for being righteous and living a good life; our rewards are the results of the grace of God, not works! God will help us meet the Leviathans of life. Any other source of hope is FALSE. Remember the little child who tried to move the large rock from his playground and finally gave up, sat down, and started to cry. His father approached and asked, "Why the tears?" After the child explained his dilemma, the father asked, "Have you tried everything?" "Of course," said the little child. "No, you haven't," the father interrupted. "You haven't asked me!" Together they removed the rock! Let's be overcomers today, not overwhelmed!

> "Hope for the Christian is a certainty, because its basis is Christ." *–Julie Ackerman Link*

~ 19 ~

Psalm 16:9 (NKJV*) – Therefore, my heart is glad, and my glory rejoices; My flesh also will rest in hope [heart, body, and soul are filled with joy].*

Remember when the logo of the YMCA/YWCA was a triangle? Each section of the triangle contained a word—body, mind, spirit. This organization was concerned for the three dimensions of life. It was what many considered a "holistic ministry." The psalmist today is reminding us that our hope influences each of these dimensions of our life. David, the author of the psalm, wants to remind his readers that God will help us face life and death. God is the God of body, mind, and spirit. Our physical, mental, and spiritual needs are met today because we trust in hope.

Is it any wonder that the Lord Jesus reminded us that we are to love the Lord with all our heart, mind, and soul? Physically, mentally, and spiritually we are to be in love with God. One of the great struggles of the soul is the turn from loving self to loving God. Humanly speaking, we have many love affairs that bring us despair and not hope. Expectation of success, therefore, is directly related to who/what we love. But in the New Testament, Jesus actually gives four dimensions of love—He adds strength! Let's look at them today.

On Valentine's Day millions of cards and boxes of candy are given to express physical (romantic) love. Often a heart-shaped image carries the phrase, "I love you." It is an expression of emotional attraction and commitment. Jesus challenges us to love the Lord emotionally—with joy, excitement, commitment. But of course this is just one dimension. He wants us to love Him mentally. Commit our brain to the Lord; love Him with our intellect. I have met a number of Christians who seem to leave their brains outside of the church—"I just live by faith" is their mantra. But Jesus wants us to deepen our faith by exercising the brain.

Of course we are to love the Lord with all our soul. We are to be "soul people." We can emotionally and intellectually love the Lord and yet miss the spiritual commitment with our soul. After all, the soul is going to live forever, so we need to feed it with worship, prayer, promise, and the Word. Can you see how His spiritual hope is to every dimension of life? Now we can complete our love affair with God by loving Him with all our strength. That's right—STRENGTH—physical, mental, and spiritual muscles need to be built up every day. It's time to work out in all these areas, get built up—lose the flab of spiritual in-activity. Then we can this very day know what the psalmist meant when he wrote: "My heart is glad, and my glory rejoices; my flesh also will rest in hope."

"Hope springs eternal in the human breast; man never is, but always to be blest." –*Alexander Pope*

~ 20 ~

Psalm 22:9 (KJV) – *"But thou art he that took me out of the womb: thou didst make me hope when I was upon my mother's breasts."*

Psalm 22 begins with the words that Jesus repeated from the cross: "My God, my God, why hast Thou forsaken Me?" It starts off as the lament of someone who feels totally deserted by God. "I am a worm, not a man, a reproach of men and despised by the people. All those who see me laugh at me, shake their heads, and mock my trusting in God." How appropriate for Jesus to remember this psalm as He is crucified. There are times in life that we could echo those words and cry out to God in a hopeless condition.

But our study offers a glimpse into the author's rebuttal to his own feelings, "You [Lord] took me out of the womb . . . yes from the beginning of my life you have been with me." Stop and meditate on that thought for a moment. For Jesus it was that night in a stable in Bethlehem; for me it was a hospital in Salem, New Jersey. For all my older brothers and sisters it was the kitchen of our house. (I was special.) The important point— our hope is based on the God of creation being with us from the beginning.

The psalmist is at complete odds with Richard Dawkins, the controversial Oxford University professor billed by many as the "world's most famous atheist." In a debate with Archbishop of Canterbury Rowan Williams, Dawkins conceded a small bit of doubt that there was no such thing as a creator; the evolutionary biologist quickly added that he was "6.9 out of seven" certain of his long-standing atheist beliefs. "I think the probability of a supernatural creator existing [is] very, very low," he said. Dawkins, author of The God Delusion and other bestsellers, is a leader of the "new atheist" movement that aggressively challenges belief in God and religion.

The psalmist believes God creates and sustains life. He notes: "Thou didst make me hope when I was on my mother's breast." Life for the newborn was sustained by nourishment from his mother—she provided the milk, and God provided the hope. Read the closing verses of Psalm 22 and you will know what that kind of hope can do—especially verse 24—" For he hath not despised nor abhorred the affliction of the afflicted; neither hath he hid his face from him; but when he cried unto him, he heard."

Today, revisit the cross. Take time to visualize our Savior dying for our sins. Think of how hopeless it seemed—how the enemy had won. Hear Jesus repeat this psalm in His agony. But then remember those glorious words of hope that followed "It is Finished" —"Father, into thy hands I commend my spirit." From the manger to the cross to the empty tomb—the path of hope.

"This is all my hope and peace; nothing but the blood of Jesus." *–Gospel song*

~ 21 ~

Psalm 31:24 (TLB) – *"Be of good courage and he shall strengthen your heart –all ye that hope in the Lord. [So cheer up! Take courage if you are depending upon the Lord.]"*

Courage and hope—a great combination. The psalmist has written this verse at the conclusion of a cry for deliverance from danger and trouble. Many think that David wrote this psalm during his time of persecution by Saul. Others believe it was written even later, possibly during the time of David's son Absalom's rebellion. Either of those experiences would be a challenge to faith, and that is exactly why we need to study the verse today. David takes us from prayer, to self-encouragement, to the causes of his trouble, to a profession of faith, to praising God, and finally to courage and hope! And all this in one psalm.

Our Lord Jesus spoke of courage. His positive words have helped me during some difficult times. "Be of good cheer [courage]. I have overcome the world." Think back with me to the cowardly lion in the motion picture *The Wizard of Oz*. Can you believe, one long weekend as an usher in a theater I watched that movie over twenty times? I knew by heart the entire script, especially the lion's dialogue. "Courage, courage, courage. I need courage." He wanted to see the wizard for one purpose— to become a courageous lion. We can have courage and hope when we belong to the Overcomer!

I was taken, one day, before a judge and chief detective of our local state troopers. Six of our boys had been in serious trouble. Our boys' home was in the formative stages and we were still learning. These boys stole from a store in our little community, and I was fearful it would mean the death of the Ranch ministry.

"Are you forcing Jesus on these boys?" was the question from the judge. "It seems you need more controls out there and less religion," added the detective. We were in a tiny office, and it was so dark I felt like it was incarceration and final judgment all combined. Only the Lord could give me the courage and "expectation of success" at the moment. I felt like Paul before King Agrippa, so I gave a positive witness for the Lord and said we would go back and improve the program.

That was nearly fifty years ago. The judge and detective are now deceased. The boys are all adults. Our ministry has continued to grow and be blessed. I am convinced God is still delivering us each day and giving us courage and hope. How about you? Here are some great suggestions on staying strong: 1) Keep only cheerful friends. Grouches pull you down. Stay close to brothers and sisters in Christ. 2) Keep learning. Never let the brain be idle. Spend more time in the Word. 3) Laugh often and loud. Rejoice in the Lord always. 4) Tears happen (even Jesus wept). Endure grief and move on. 5) Cherish your health. If it is good, maintain it; if unstable, improve it; if beyond help, see a doctor. The body is still the temple of God. 6) Don't take guilt trips. Take a trip to church and find the answer to guilt. 7) Love people, love the Lord, love yourself, and remember life is not measured by the number of breaths we take but by the moments that take our breath away.

"I am prepared for the worst but always hope for the best." *–Benjamin Disraeli*

~ 22 ~

Psalm 33:18 (KJV) – *"Behold, the eye of the Lord is upon those that fear him, upon them that hope in his mercy [who rely on his steadfast love]."*

Now we find fear and hope combined. Often fear is presented as a negative, but here we see it in concert with hope. Fear can be a very positive emotion if used in the context of fearing God for the right reasons. I've counseled many who let fear become a sickness and phobia that is not the fear of the Bible.

It was the month of August, and the Ranch was wracked by a vicious summer storm. Rain fell violently on the campus, causing severe flooding. In addition, thunder and lightning were awesome. Our boys and staff huddled in the cottages, hoping that it would soon pass. Fear gripped the hearts of even our most "macho" teenagers. As the storm was subsiding, there came a loud band from the heavens and what seemed to be a simultaneous flash of light. It was obvious that something had been struck by a bolt from the storm. Anxiously, boys and staff peered out to see an electrical transformer and pole on fire. It looked like a Fourth of July celebration, but under the conditions it was cause for great concern. The local fire company was called, and the problem was soon under control.

Later, houseparents told me of some of their experiences during the near catastrophe. A number of boys in each cottage "sought the Lord." It was the beginning of a spiritual revival. The boys had heaven scared into them. We turned this into a positive experience of fearing the Lord and hope in His mercy. That's the only way any experience like that can be meaningful and lasting. Maybe you have had a similar fearful experience. Build upon that negative and make it a positive in your spiritual growth.

"That's God"

Have you ever been just sitting there and all of a sudden you feel like doing something nice for someone you care for? That's God. He talks to you through the Holy Spirit.

Have you ever been down and out and nobody seems to be around for you to talk to? That's God. He wants you to talk to Him.

Have you ever been in a situation and had no clue how it was going to get better, until now when you look back on it? That's God. He passes us through tribulation to see a brighter day.

In all that we do, we should totally give HIM thanks, and our blessings will continue to multiply.
Don't tell GOD how big your storm is; tell the storm how big your GOD is!

"Beware how you take away hope from another human being." –*Oliver Wendell Holmes*

~ 23 ~

Psalm 33:22 (KJV) – *"Let Thy mercy, O Lord, be upon us as, according as we hope in Thee [for our hopes are in you alone]."*

This psalm has no title. It was possibly written by David, but we have no authority for that. The psalm begins with a burst of joy, "Rejoice in the Lord" and concludes with a prayer of confidence and hope. In between is the oft-quoted verse: "Blessed is the nation whose God is the Lord and the people whom he hath chosen for his own inheritance." I used that verse on the foundation for a message I shared on the National Day of Prayer, but the message extends beyond the nation to our own personal level.

Today we want to take special note that we can hope in the Lord, because we know of His mercy and goodness toward us. Experiences of the past give us an "expectation of success" for the future. Years ago I memorized a quote that I used in high school while running for student council president. I have no idea who I quoted, but its meaning is still very relevant. Speaking to the student body in high school, I concluded my appeal for their votes by saying, "The best way to judge a person's actions in the future is by his performance in the past." I'm not sure that phrase helped me win the election, but it has stuck with me over the years. We have over two thousand years of biblical history to look back on. We know that God has been faithful to His people in the past, and we can trust Him into our future.

A friend sent me the following thought-provoking illustration. Each of these creatures has a message for us:

The Buzzard, Bat, and Bumblebee

Buzzard – If you put a buzzard in a 6' by 8' pen that is entirely open at the top, the bird, in spite of its ability to fly, will be an absolute prisoner. The reason is that a buzzard always begins a flight from the ground with a run of ten to twelve feet. Without space to run, as is its habit, it will not even attempt to fly, but will remain a prisoner for life in a small jail with no top.

Bat – The ordinary bat that flies around at night, a remarkably nimble creature in the air, cannot take off from a level place. If it is placed on the floor or flat ground, all it can do is shuffle about helplessly and painfully until it reaches some slight elevation from which it can throw itself into the air. Then, at once, it takes off like a flash.

Snapshots

"High hopes nothin'. I've got kids to feed."

Bumblebee – A bumblebee, if dropped into an open tumbler, will lie there until it dies, unless it is taken out. It never sees the means of escape at the top, but persists in trying to find some way out through the sides near the bottom. It will seek a way where none exists, until it completely destroys itself.

People – In many ways, we are like the buzzard, the bat, and the bumblebee. We struggle about with all our problems and frustrations, never realizing that all we have to do is look up. Sorrow looks back, worry looks around, but faith looks up. Live simply, love generously, care deeply, speak kindly, and trust in our God who loves us.

May your troubles be less, your blessings more, and may nothing but happiness come through your door.

Now take time to read the entire psalm, and it will be a blessing. Review in your mind how God's mercy has blessed you in the past, and then approach today with hope!

"The word which God has written on the brow of every man is hope." *–Victor Hugo*

~ 24 ~

Psalm 38:15 (KJV) – *"For in thee, O Lord, do I hope: thou wilt hear, O Lord my God [for I am waiting, O Lord; come and protect me]."*

This psalm is attributed to an "unknown sufferer." Many churches have used this as a special responsive reading for Ash Wednesday. Some call it a penitential psalm (a feeling sorry for sin, repentance). Whoever the writer is, he is hurting from a sense of God's displeasure, the loss of friends, fear of harm from his enemies, and suffering from health problems. To make matters worse, this is a result of the believer's own sin. Suffering can be the result of sin. We make bad choices, we rebel against God, and we reap negative consequences. Billy Graham defined sin as "missing the mark." Imagine we are equipped with a target, a bow, and an arrow. We take our position and focus on the bull's-eye. Carefully we are hoping to hit the target, especially the bull's-eye. But we miss! We miss everything we had hoped to hit. That, simply speaking, is our failure to live up to our walk with God.

But now enter HOPE. You would think that all this failure would cause a person to give up. But enter HOPE. The writer will not despair, will not capitulate to these adversaries; instead he clings to God. Exit despair, enter HOPE. Can you relate to the writer? His bones were aching; he had a sense of burning in his body, palpitations of the heart, was tired all over, and even his sight was failing. Enter HOPE! It takes more than medication, more than exercise, more than psycho-therapy—it takes hope.

Today we will relate hope to a slow dance. (I know some of you Baptists can't relate to any kind of dancing, but give it a try.) The analogy is a good one for a picture of life void of all the rushing and stress that many of us endure each day. So put on the music, a nice slow song, and enjoy the dance.

Have you ever watched kids on a merry-go-round or listened to the rain slapping on the ground?

Ever followed a butterfly's erratic flight or gazed at the sun into the fading night? You better slow down. Don't dance so fast. Time is short. The music won't last.
Do you run through each day on the fly? When you ask, "How are you?" do you hear the reply?

When the day is done, do you lie in your bed with the next hundred chores running through your head?

You'd better slow down. Don't dance so fast. Time is short. The music won't last.

Ever told your child, we'll do it tomorrow? And in your haste, not see his sorrow?

Ever lost touch, let a good friendship die 'cause you never had time to call and say, "Hi"?

You'd better slow down. Don't dance so fast. Time is short. The music won't last.

When you run so fast to get somewhere, you miss half the fun of getting there. When you worry and hurry through your day, it is like an unopened gift, thrown away.

Life is not a race. Do take it slower. Hear the music before the song is over.

"Most of the important things in the world have been accomplished by people who have kept on trying when there seemed to be no hope at all." *–Dale Carnegie*

~ 25 ~

Psalm 39:7 (NKJV) *–"And now, Lord, what do I wait for? My hope is in You."*

Ever feel like complaining? Ever become disgruntled with life? You are not alone. This psalm is written by someone who is prepared to list his grievances about life and then decides to remain silent. Fearful of repercussions from his enemies, he makes a vain attempt to suppress everything negative. Note the opening verse. But human nature quickly dictates his course, and a dramatic change takes place. All the suppressed anger and frustration is unleashed.

It is important to remember that there is a therapeutic value to "letting it go." We used to take it to an extreme in our counseling with young people. Periodically, our counseling staff would have a child scream out all their bitterness and anger, even to the extent of taking a boy outside the office and permitting him to rant and rave until exhausted. Obviously, the results of such therapy were limited and an alternative plan had to be devised. "Hope therapy" is better than "scream therapy."

How To Mend a Broken Heart
How do you mend a broken heart? What do you do when you've got a broken heart? Here are four steps that will help you up that mountain:
1. Occupy   2. Gratify   3. Sanctify   4. Glorify

Occupy – Occupy your time; don't sit around moping. Do something. Idleness is the soil of self-pity and depression. Get busy. The best thing that you can do is to do something that helps others. It's a universal principle that when you start focusing on helping others, your own problems are diminished. Don't just stand there, DO SOMETHING!

Gratify – write a list of things you like, then pick three of those things and put those things in your life—now. Make sure you can afford them and that they aren't harmful. When our hearts are broken, we often deprive ourselves of the things we enjoy. Make an effort to put enjoyment in your life.

Sanctify – Do good. Don't return evil for evil, hurt for hurt, pain for pain. Don't wish something horrible would happen to the other person. Hope for their good fortune in your world. The easiest way to forget someone is to truly wish them well.

Glorify – Life is not over. You can live without them. Not only can you live without them, you can live even happier without them. It is a matter of perspective. Even with the negative in your world at the moment, there is something to be thankful for. There is plenty to be thankful for, actually. Give God the glory for what you have. You can't be sad and thankful at the same time. Tell heartbreak to move over.

David is assigned the authorship of the psalm. After writing it, he gave it to a choir master to put to music. It is filled with poetic beauty, but beyond that is a great spiritual truth. After the outburst, there is a question: "What do I wait for? My hope is in You." At the end of the complaining, David throws himself into the arms of God and submits himself to God. Please remember today, when your mother and father forsake you—hope in God. When you feel like complaining, when you are disgruntled with life, when you are frustrated—hope then in God.

> "Never deprive someone of hope; it might be all they have." –H. Jackson Brown Jr.

~ 26 ~

Psalm 42:5 (KJV) – *"Why art thou cast down, O my soul? and why art thou disquieted in me? hope thou in God."*

50

Psalms didn't just happen—they are the result of events and experiences in the life of the author. Psalm 42 was written by David as a result of a difficult family "dysfunction." As we mentioned earlier, David's son, Absalom, decided to overthrow David as king and lead a major rebellion. Now all of us know bad family "challenges" but nothing quite as serious as this. Absalom wanted to kill his father and replace him on the throne. Talk about palace intrigue. No wonder David writes, "Why are you cast down my soul; why are you so upset?" David used the phrase "cast down" because as a shepherd he had seen sheep get cast down. So heavy with mud and defecation their woolen coats matted, they would be cast down and unable to get up.

Events in our families can have positive or negative effects upon our walk with the Lord. The foundation for David's trouble was laid before Absalom's birth. David had married a woman strictly for political convenience—she was a foreign leader's daughter whose country was at war with Israel. This was supposed to bring peace between the countries, but it brought another woman into David's harem, and she gave birth to Absalom. Another child in a palace full of different siblings from different marriages.

I remember the story of the caseworker who found a mother living with five boys, all with the first name Daniel. She asked the mother, "Why did you name them the same name?" The mother responded, "It is easy to call them all at once with the same name." The caseworker asked her, "Suppose you want just one in particular?" The mother said, "I call them by their last name." Sad, but true.

In our ministry to troubled families, we have seen this repeated over and over again. Many children with different fathers and mothers trying to exist as a family. The challenges are many. Today would be a special time to pray for the family, our family, whatever the position or negative aspects. David reached a point in his struggles that he must hope in God. As you will remember, Absalom was killed in battle. David's major military leader found him hanging by his hair in a tree and inflicted a deadly blow. When David was given the news, he cried: "Absalom, my son Absalom. Would that I had died for you." Too late, David!

The hope for our family is the One who died for us. Jesus died for the stable and the unstable families. The down and outers and the up and outers. He can help the dysfunctional family to function. If you are cast down today with a troubled family or know of such a family, take time right now to pray for each person and each situation. It will help us from being upset to having hope.

"Faith thrives when there is no hope but God." *–Ernest Gordan, POW, World War II*

~ 27 ~

Psalm 43:5 (NIV) – *"Why, my soul, are you downcast? Why so disturbed within me? Put your hope in God."*

Yes, this is a repeat of the verse Psalm 42. There is a close connection between the two, as they were written by the same author. Because it is a continuation, the repetition of its use is natural and fits into the thoughts written by David during this time of conflict. The NIV translation makes it so very clear. David, having worked with sheep as a boy, knew that this animal can be "cast down." A sheep becomes cast down when it lays in a rut in the ground for a long period of time. The rut gets deeper and deeper, and sometimes the sheep's wool becomes matted with dirt. The weight of the wool and the depth of the rut make it impossible for the sheep to get up by itself. It becomes "cast down." Is it possible David was referring to this as he repeats this question? He was cast down with the "ruts and weight" of the world. Note this special reading about being overworked.

Overworked

Do you ever feel like this person? For a couple years I've been blaming it on lack of sleep, not enough sunshine, too much pressure from my job, earwax buildup, poor blood, or anything else I could think of. But now I found out the real reason: I'm tired because I'm overworked—here's why!

The population of this country is 300 million. One hundred fifty million are retired. That leaves 100 million to do the work.

There are 85 million in school, which leaves 48 million to do the work. Of this, 29 million are employed by the federal government, leaving 19 million to do the work.

2.8 million are in the armed forces, which leaves 16.2 million to do the work.

Take from the total the 14,800,00 people who work for state and city governments. That leaves 1.4 million to do the work.

At any given time 188,000 people are in hospitals, leaving 1,212,000 to do the work. There are 1,211,998 people in prisons. That leaves just two people to do the work—you and me.

I have found myself in ruts and cast down. Sometimes the rut has become comfortable and then I start putting on the weight of the world. For years there was a sign on the Alaskan Highway that read, "Choose your rut carefully. You will be in it for the next 200 miles." The highway was still undeveloped, and that sign could have been literally true. Others have said that a rut is a grave with the ends kicked out. It is important to get out of the rut and turn our attention again to hope—hope in God.

> "The ninety and nine are with dreams, content, but the hope of the world made new, is the hundredth man who is grimly bent on making those dreams come true."
> *–Edgar Allen Poe*

~ 28 ~

Psalm 71:5 (NKJV) – *"For You are my hope, O Lord GOD; You are my trust from my youth."*

This is another psalm attributed to David. David is king of Israel at this time. He is wealthy and famous, but he knows deep down he is spiritually poor and needs help. He reminds us that he has trusted in the Lord from his childhood. Someone had started him in the right direction. But we find David vacillating between praise and complaint in the entire psalm. Our verse of the day centers in his hope that can be traced all the way back to his childhood. Often we are the result of our childhood hopes, or lack of them.

Most of the young people we minister to have no such history. Often they have only heard the name of the Lord used as a curse word. Religious faith at the most has been on the peripheral of their family life. One of our young people, remembering his father's abuse of God's name, wrote a short tract titled "God's last name ain't damn." Those of us who have trusted in the Lord since our youth are in the minority and are blessed. Hope can grow in our life from childhood to adulthood.

If I Had My Life To Live Over

If I had my life to live over,
I'd try to make more mistakes next time;
I would relax more; I'd be sillier this next trip;
Limber up more.
I would take more trips; I would be crazier.
I would climb more mountains, swim more rivers, and watch more sunsets;
I would do more walking and looking –
I would eat more ice cream and less beans –
I would have more actual problems and less imaginary ones.
You see, I've been one of those people who lives life very sensibly—hour after hour, day after day.
Oh, I've had some wonderful moments, but if I had to do it over again, I'd have more of them.
I'd stop living so many years ahead of each day.
I've been one of those people who would never go anywhere without a gargle, a thermometer, a rain coat, an aspirin, and a parachute.
Yes, I think I'd go more places, do more things, and travel lighter than I have.

I would start going barefoot earlier in the spring and stay that way into the fall.

I'd play hookey more; I would ride on more merry-go-rounds; I'd stop to pick daisies..

Religious testimony of a monk: "I would commit my life to the Lord early—so I could enjoy every blessed day He gives me."

Take time now to review your life. Think of those who helped build your "expectation of success." Thank God now for each family member, teacher, minister, neighbor, Sunday school teacher, and others that helped give you spiritual nourishment. If you had your life to live over, I know you would make it more "hope centered."

> "The natural flights of the human mind are not from pleasure to pleasure, but from hope to hope." *–Samuel Johnson*

~ 29 ~

Psalm 71:14 (KJV) – *"I will hope continually."* (TLB) *"I will keep expecting you to help me."*

Like so many of the psalms, this one alternates between complaint and praise. There is nothing new here, as we find complaining mixed with prayer and thanksgiving (sounds very human)! The verse we study today is considered transitional, taking the author from complaint to HOPE. It's as though he has listed concerns in his life and says, "As for me, I will hope." In fact, he says, "I will add all my past praises to these and even look for more in the future." Now that is HOPE.

We published our first brochure on Ranch Hope before there was any ranch. We published information about what we hoped to do. There were pictures of plans conceived by our architect, and on the cover was a view of the lake we bordered. I wrote the copy describing what we were going to do, not what we were doing. When I reread it now, many years and experiences later, I am amazed. We were either very ignorant or very presumptuous in our planning. But then I am blessed by a key phrase we published on the opening page of the brochure. "We who would expect great things from God must attempt great things for God." I know now that hope is neither ignorant nor presumptuous. It is an "expectation of success." Look at this reading on 7-UP (not the soft drink):

"7-UP"

Wake up! Decide to have a good day. "This is the day the Lord hath made; let us rejoice and be glad in it" (Psalm 118:24).

Dress Up! The best way to dress up is to put on a smile. A smile is an inexpensive way to improve your looks. "The Lord does not look at the things man looks at; man looks at the outward appearance, but the Lord looks at the heart" (1 Samuel 16:17).

Shut Up! Say nice things and learn to listen. God gave us two ears and one mouth, so He must have meant for us to do twice as much listening as talking. "He who guards his soul" (Proverbs 13:3).

Stand Up! for what you believe in. Stand for something, or you will fall for anything. "Let us not weary in doing good; for at the proper time, we will reap a harvest if we do not give up. Therefore, as we have opportunity, let us do good" (Galatians 6:9–10).

Look Up! to the Lord. "I can do everything through Christ who strengthens me" (Philippians 4:13).

Reach Up! for something higher. "Trust in the Lord with all your heart, and lean not unto your own understanding. In all your ways, acknowledge Him, and He will direct your path" (Proverbs 3:5–6).

Lift Up! your prayers. "Do not worry about anything; instead PRAY ABOUT EVERYTHING" (Philippians 4:6).

In the *Living Bible*, the translator helps this verse come alive today. Note: "I will keep expecting you to help me." Today we display that thought on the refrigerator door of our mind. "When there's life, there's hope!" –*Marcus Tullius Cicero*

~ 30 ~

Psalm 78:7 – *"In this way each generation has been able to obey his laws and to set its hope anew on God and not forget his glorious miracles...and hear his commands."*

The Jews believed in passing on the law of Moses from generation to generation. Every generation was to be reminded who they were and where they had come from. Notice that hope was to be new because it was built on God, his miracles, and the keeping of His commandments. What a foundation for every generation!

Each generation does pass on a message to its descendants. It can be a message of hope (confidence) or one of despair. It can be one of expectation of success or failure. Sometimes it is done in dramatic events, or often by more subtle influences. But a message will be communicated. "Setting our hope anew on God" is a great message for every generation.

Sometimes it can be reversed—grandchildren can pass on a message of hope to us! We find hope in some unusual ways. Consider this illustration by Pamela Perry Blaine:

One evening at suppertime my granddaughter Amanda was in the high chair and I went over to the kitchen counter to fill her plate. Her mother put three small crackers on her high chair tray to give her something to eat while I fixed her plate. I watched as she bowed her head and touched the first cracker with her index finger and said, "Amen cracker." She touched the next cracker and said, "Amen cracker," and then she went to the last cracker, touched it, and again said, "Amen cracker." She thought the tiny crackers were her supper, so she was saying her prayers. Amanda has figured out that prayers have an "amen" in them, but sometimes she gets the "amen" at the beginning instead of at the end of her prayers.

I got to thinking about the word "amen," and I found that in Hebrew the word amen means to confirm, and it is spoken to state, "So be it." When we end our prayers with "amen," we are reaffirming our dedication to God. Sometimes church members or congregations say amen to show confirmation or agreement when something powerful is spoken from the Word of God.

Amanda's prayer might seem very simple, but maybe she wasn't so far off in what she was doing because she would have been confirming her dedication to God first instead of at the end. At any rate, we can gain wisdom from "the mouths of babes." I learned several things from Amanda and her "amen crackers."

- I learned that prayer should be a priority.
- I learned that whatever is on my "plate," I should be thankful for it.
- I learned I should keep it simple and specific.
- I learned to have faith and trust God even when all I have is three crackers.
- I learned it is best to tend to my own crackers that have been provided for me and allow God to fill my plate.
- I learned to be patient. Even if I'm sitting in a high chair, I can't see what is going on in God's kitchen from where I sit.
- I learned to thank God for the small things and not complain, even if all I have is crackers.
- I learned it doesn't matter if you get the prayer backward; God hears our hearts.

Have you thanked God for the crackers in your life?
–*Pamela Perry Blaine*

"Where there is no vision, there is no hope." –*George Washington Carver*

~ 31 ~

Psalm 119:43 – *"May I never forget your words, for they are my only hope..."*

This is a long psalm. It contains 21 traits of being blessed, 15 actions performed by God, 30 vows, 30 reasons for vows, 70 requests, 18 secrets of victory, 61 testimonies, 62 facts about the Word, 22 reasons God is happy, 198 references to God's Word, and 610 personal pronouns. Notice today the I and My because this has been called the "Psalm of the Word of God." We will relate this to HOPE.

The words of God (contained in the Word of God) are my only hope. Do you believe that? Words, words, words. As one popular advertisement said, "We are what we speak. People know us by the words we use." Words are important, and the psalmist knew he must be filled with the words of God if he was to be hopeful.

Notice how the meaning of words change. When I was young, the word tough meant "that's your problem." Later, young people used it to refer to something that was "cool." Think of how words like hot dog, turkey, gay, swell, gross, etc. changed from generation to generation. Yet the "Word of God" gives hope because the words do not change. His Word remains the same.

Presidents of the United States have recognized this important fact. At their inauguration, did you know that each president selects a Bible verse and an attendant stands holding the Bible? The president seals his oath with a kiss upon his favorite verse of Scripture. Here are some of the favorites:

Abraham Lincoln, March 4, 1861, chose Revelation 16:7, "And I heard another out of the altar say, even Lord God Almighty, true and righteous are thy judgments."

Chester A. Arthur, September 20, 1881, selected Psalm 31:1–3, "In thee, O Lord, do I put my trust . . . lead me and guide me."

Theodore Roosevelt, September 14, 1901, selected James 2:22–23, "But be ye doers of the word, and not hearers only."

Harry S. Truman, April 12, 1945, picked Matthew 5:9, "Blessed are the peacemakers: for they shall be called the children of God."

Dwight D. Eisenhower, January 20, 1953, chose 2 Chronicles 7:14, "If my people, which are called by my name, shall humble themselves and pray."

So take time today to read the "long psalm," and meditate on the words as they point you to the Word. Make the message important to your personal pronoun. In a world where everything is changing, it is a welcome relief to never forget His word of hope. Is there a passage that you might select at your swearing-in ceremony? Just a thought.

> "Hope is the word which God has written on the brow of every man" *–Victor Hugo*

~ 32 ~

Psalm 119:49–56 (TLB) – *"Never forget your promises to me –your servant—for they are my only hope."*

Are you looking for "songs in the night"? Many have called this section of Psalm 119 (verses 49–56) just such songs. These songs will do us more good than the most recent top 10, or the golden oldies we listen to, or even some of the new gospel classics. God gives these songs. He is the composer and arranger, and editor and publisher. Note this verse is centered in HOPE— and that hope is centered in the promises from God.

People keep or break promises. Everyone has had both experiences. You can imagine the experiences we have had with young people. George looked at me, and with all the innocence of his fifteen years, said, "I learned my lesson and you can trust me to go home this weekend." George had made a profession of faith in Christ, and we were ready to put him to the test. After all, he gave us his word. One day into his weekend pass, we were called by the state police. George had shoplifted at a local department store. I had to pick him up in Atlantic City and return him to the Ranch. The ride home was quiet. Finally I broke his silence. "Why, George? You promised. You gave your word." George's response was classic, "I thought if I became a Christian, God would protect me from the cops." So much for the promises, so much for his word.

Thank God my hope was not built on that experience or many like it. Young people, and all people, can learn from such stories. Our "songs in the night" will be based on His Word and His Promises. Consider the following story:

Joachim Neander is not a common household name. If I told you he wrote the stirring hymn "Praise to the Lord, the Almighty," you would at least have some frame of reference. He became a Christian at the age of twenty and died ten short years later. During that ten-year period he was a strong Christian witness, served youth as a German high school teacher, and wrote additional hymns. One such hymn, not as well known, is "All My Hope on God Is Founded." It contains a promise worth remembering—though the towers and temples of this world fall to dust, we can forward our hope on God, who alone is worthy of trust (paraphrase). Place that "song" in your memory bank as we see the towers and temples all around us falling to dust. If it was true for the world of Joachim Neander, so it is true for our generation. Tonight if you have trouble sleeping, turn to Psalm 119 and reread verses 49–56. Focus on each verse; it will be music to your ears and a comfort to your soul. Sleep well!

> "We must free ourselves of the hope that the sea will ever rest, We must learn to sail in high winds!"
> –*Aristotle Onassis*

~ 33 ~

Psalm 119:81 (NIV) – *"My soul faints with longing for your salvation, but I have put my hope in your word."*

Ever faint? It is not a good experience. Doctors tell us there are all kinds of reasons for such an event. It could be a drop in blood pressure or an increase; it could be some trauma to the head, or some unexplained shock to our physical or emotional system. But I doubt that it is because we are "longing for God's salvation." Not that it hasn't happened or couldn't happen, but it certainly is not the norm. Yet the psalmist writes that it has happened to him.

Keep in mind how very long this psalm is (176 verses). Throughout this compilation of meditations, the writer is focusing on the excellencies of the Word of God. He really delights in the law of the Lord. The word is not some add-on to his life; it is his life. Everything he is about is about the law. In reading through the many verses, we know he had staked his life and security on the law. He values God's word over any material possession. Is it any wonder he states, "My soul faints with longing for your salvation, but I have put my hope in your word."

No one who longs for and even faints for salvation will go unheard. Build your hope on that. In a novel assignment, a fifth-grade teacher asked her students to look at TV commercials and see if they could use ads for ideas to communicate with God. The results were interesting. Here are a few:

> God is like *Bounty* – He is the quicker-picker-upper. He can handle a tough job, and He won't fall apart on you.
> God is like *Allstate* – You are in good hands with Him.
> God is like *Walmart* – He has everything.
> God is like *Tide* – He gets the stains out that others leave behind.
> God is like *Hallmark* – He cares enough to send His very best (my favorite).
> God is like *Bayer Aspirin* – He works miracles.
> God is like *GE.* – He brings good things to life.

The fifth-grade class gave us a great message. In a simplistic look at TV ads, they gave us a message of hope. But remember, it is predicated on a serious study of the Word.

> "Hope is like the Energizer bunny—it helps us keep going, going, going!"

~ 34 ~

Psalm 119:114 (NKJV) – *"You are my hiding place and my shield; I hope in Your word."*

Joy Gage, writing in the devotional the Upper Room, tells of a tiny town in Arizona called Hope. In the winter, if you drive through the little town, you will see hundreds of recreational vehicles, trailers, RVs, and pop-up tents covering the landscape. For four months of the year the town is home to visitors escaping the cold. Yet if you visit in the summertime, you will see a main street that is mostly boarded up. Regardless of when you visit, however, as you drive out of town, you will see a sign that reads "You're now beyond Hope." The psalmist that penned today's verse knew he was never beyond hope because God was his shield, his hiding place, and he hoped in God's Word.

Psalm 119 is a collection of meditations on the excellencies of the word of God. Throughout the 166 verses we are reminded of the Law, the ordinances, the statutes, the commandments, and the judgment of God. It is a compilation of the Word and words of God. This particular verse could be something David or another military leader composed—emphasis on a hiding place and a shield.

Picture with me a military person under duress in battle looking for a cave or other place of refuge. Now associate that with battles we endure in life and needing a hiding place. It is the Lord who becomes that place for us, and we rush to Him for safety. It may be a "fox hole" of faith or a bomb shelter, but it becomes our shield from anything that would destroy us. One anonymous author said it so well:

A Memo from God

I am God. Come to my hiding place. Today I will be handling your problems. If life happens to deliver a situation to you that you cannot handle, do not attempt to resolve it. Kindly put it in the SFGTD (something for God to do) box. Once the matter is place into the box, do not hold on to it or remove it. If it is a situation that you think you are capable of handling, please consult me in prayer to be sure it is the proper resolution. Because I do not sleep nor do I slumber, there is no need for you to lose any sleep. Rest, my child. If you need to contact me, read my word and pray.

Be happy with what you have. Should you find it hard to get to sleep tonight, just remember the homeless family who has no bed to lie in.

Should you have a bad day at work, think of the man who has been out of work for years.

Should you despair over a relationship gone bad, think of the person who has never known what it's like to love and to be loved in return.

Should you notice a new gray hair in the mirror, think of the cancer patient in chemo who wishes she had hair to examine.

Should you find yourself at a loss and pondering what life is all about, asking, "What is my purpose?" be thankful. There are those who didn't live long enough to get that opportunity.

Should you find yourself the victim of other people's bitterness, ignorance, smallness, or insecurities, re-member, things could be worse. You could be them!

"Hope is not a way out; it is a way through." –*Anonymous*

~ 35 ~

Psalm 130:5 – *"My soul waits – and in His word I put my trust . . . O Israel hope in the Lord."*

There are a few advantages to growing old (not many, but a few). The late Will Rogers was one of the greatest humorists our nation has ever known. He once wrote, "Eventually you will reach a point when you stop lying about your age and start bragging about it." Then he added, "The older we get, the fewer things seem worth waiting for in life." For the writer of Psalm 130, hope comes from learning to wait, whatever our age, and especially to wait on the Lord.

This psalm is a poem of repentance (a change from being self-centered to God-centered). The writer is despairing over the sin in his life and he wants to be forgiven. If we were to break this down into an outline, it would be as follows: (a) verses 1 and 2–a call for God's mercy, (b) verses 3 and 4–knowing God forgives, (c) verses 5 and 6 –expecting God to forgive, (d) –a call for the mercy of God on everyone. So today, thousands of years later, we have an outline to follow for our repentance. No need to despair over sin, no need to wait to repent, we place our hope in His Word—we are forgiven!

I am blessed to know that God does not keep count of our failures, our backsliding, or our sin. God is not a bean-counting accountant that has a big ledger with plusses and minuses after our name. We do not gain forgiveness because we build up brownie points. But we do recognize how Christ's death for our sin is not to be taken lightly; beware of cheap grace.

In his book, *Gods at War,* Kyle Idleman writes about the idols that battle for our heart. He uses the analogy of a polluted stream. Someone has been dumping trash into the water until it is an ugly sight. You are on a hike and notice it. Because of your concern for the beauty of nature, you stoop down and start removing the trash. It takes nearly an hour, but as you leave, everything looks better. However, when you come back the next day, you find it once again trashed. This seems strange (garbage cannot breed), so you follow the creek upstream. You are amazed when you find the source of the problem—a garbage dump is at the head of the stream, and it empties into the passing water. If you want the stream clean, you must go to the source. So Kyle reminds us that for us to be cleaned up spiritually, we must go to the source of our pollution, the heart.

Today enter into your own confessional booth. Right where you are—right now! Talk with our loving Father. Tell Him about any pollution you want to confess. The good news is He will replace pollution with hope. Hope that we can go to the source of the problem (the heart) and be made clean.

"Hope helps get your heart back on track." *–Anonymous*

~ 36 ~

Psalm 146:5 – *"But happy is the man who has the God of Jacob as his helper, whose hope is in the Lord his God."*

Happiness is taught in the Bible. Jesus began the Sermon on the Mount with the famous beatitudes. They teach us the "be-happy attitude." Others have called these the "blessed attitudes." But it is vitally important to know that scriptural happiness is always a result of our relationship to the Lord. This is the truth taught in today's study.

Psalm 146 is called a psalm of praise. It could easily be set to music and used as a praise chorus in our church services. Note that praise and happiness are interrelated because the more we praise the Lord, the more happiness we experience. David wrote this psalm as a reminder to his generation that the God of Jacob is our keeper and source of hope.

A few years ago, I read a book listing the seven needs of youth. The author wrote about a child needing praise, security, love, status, discipline, substance (material things like clothing, food, and shelter), and spiritual help. Our society, in varying degrees, emphasizes each of these but often neglects the spiritual. In our ministry at Ranch Hope, we have attempted to make this need paramount to the others. It has been our conviction when the spiritual needs are met, the other needs can more readily be addressed. In our culture today, there is great emphasis on children being educated, having good nourishing food, and living in a home. All these are important, but we can raise a generation of youth who are academically brilliant with strong and healthy bodies living in nice suburban neighborhoods—but who have no hope, no expectation of success for their future.

Today many youth and adults are struggling with needs that cannot be humanly met. In reality, those seven needs of youth remain with us a lifetime. We don't outgrow them with aging.

The bumper sticker asked, "Have you hugged your kid today?" I wanted one printed, "Have you hugged your grandpop today?" Possibly it is time to recognize the root of our needs. Happiness for Jacob and Jesus was based on hope in the Lord. Start singing a praise chorus, and then sing it again. Let the praise of God start filling the vacuum in your life. Here is a chorus that you may not know, but the words are a blessing:

> Praise Him! Praise Him! Praise Him in the morning!
> Praise Him at the noontime!
> And Praise Him when the sun goes down!
> Happy is the person who praises God morning, noon, and night.

"Man's only true happiness is to live in hope of something to be won by him, reverence something to be worshipped by him, and love something to be cherished by him forever." *–John Ruskin*

~ 37 ~

Psalm 147:11 (NIV) – *"The Lord delights in those who fear him, who put their hope in his unfailing love."*

The Lord takes pleasure (it makes Him happy) in those that fear Him, in those that hope in his mercy. Want to make God happy? It's tied to two words: fear and hope!

We don't usually think of the word hope when we think of fear. Fear seems so ominous, so negative. Hope is so encouraging and positive. But these words are part of a bigger picture. This is a psalm of praise, one of the twenty four such psalms distributed throughout the book. It begins with the words, "Praise the Lord." Then the author reminds us that God heals the broken in heart, lifts up the weak, and casts down the wicked. We are instructed to sing unto the Lord with thanksgiving. But all of this is predicated upon a deep respect (for) and hope centered in Him.

Think of the psalms as the popular songs of that day. As our young people have their "top ten" and know the words by heart, so many of these psalms were well known and memorized. It is difficult, however, to believe people will remember our "pop" songs 2400 years from now; rap will have gone the way of all flesh. (As will rock and roll, the big bands, jazz, hip hop, crooners, etc.) Of course, one of the major dichotomies between these two genres of music is today's preoccupation with romantic love. What a contrast between praising the Lord and "I love you, baby. I need you, baby. I lost you, baby. I want you back, baby!"

It is also important to note an interesting analogy included in this part of the psalm. The author speaks of the strength of horses and the legs of man. Horses were important in those days for transportation, for communication, for the military (in the book of Revelation they were symbols of war, death, famine, and hell). Horses were known for their speed, beauty, and durability. The legs of men were depended upon for obvious reasons—both important to kings and commoners. But the psalmist wants to remind everyone that the Lord is not impressed by either horses or the legs of man. To impress God to give Him pleasure, fear Him and hope in His mercy.

So we focus on two words. First, fear. Remember that the fear (respect and awe) of the Lord is the beginning of knowledge (Proverbs 1:7). If you want to grow in the knowledge of the Lord, it starts with a healthy fear (respect, reverenced awe) of God. It then moves to hoping (a great expectation) in His mercy. I saved mercy until last because I want this to be our closing emphasis. Mercy is God's compassion and kindness toward us even when we don't deserve it. We can hope in mercy because God is merciful. Put it down; underline it.

> "Hope sees the invisible, feels the intangible, and accomplishes the impossible." *–Anonymous*

~ 38 ~

Proverbs 13:12 (NKJV) – *"Hope deferred [put off] makes the heart sick, But when the desire comes, it is a tree of life."*

Ever been heartsick? Not a term used very often, but we can all relate. Obviously, the writer of Proverbs is not referring to the organ in our body called the heart. It is not a diseased artery or blocked valve he is referring to. This deals more with our emotional or spiritual condition. Situations happen in life, and when any expectation of success (hope) is delayed or put off, then we can feel heartsick. The verse is not saying I need instant gratification. Our writer is merely making an important observation. We can get tired of waiting for something we hope for. As one writer stated, "People can grow weary of persistently unmet expectations." I think all of us have been in that position.

A few years ago a young couple were about to be married. They had dated for a number of years and were deeply in love. Both active Christians, they went to their pastor and, after making arrangement for the date and place of marriage, the pastor recommended they take four weeks of counseling. Accepting his recommendation, they faithfully attended each session and completed his prescribed reading and instruction. But then the unexpected bomb dropped. The pastor left town without any warning; the church closed and was put up for sale. Talk about being heartsick, this was a major heart attack.

But a tree of life was about to bloom. I was consulted by the groom's parents to fill in. You can imagine the young couple's absolute delight. After the devastating deferment of their hope (marriage), we were able to provide a pastor and chapel for their wedding. As the couple embraced after taking vows and exchanging rings, I was blessed to bless their marriage; I became a part of healing their heartsickness. No longer heartsick, they left the chapel full of hope for a marriage centered in Christ.

A few Christian one-liners come to mind…

• Don't let your worries get the best of you; remember Moses started out as a basket case.
• When you get to your wits end, you will find God lives there.
• God promises a safe landing, not a calm passage.
• The task ahead of us is never as great as the power behind us.
• A Christian should be standing on the promises, not sitting on the premises! AMEN.

Today you may remember an experience of deferred hope. Or possibly you are witnessing an experience right now. It is time to focus on the healing process—to believe that God will meet your desire through people or circumstances. Little did that young couple know that God would use someone originally totally out of the picture to be their tree of life. Healing does come.

"Hope is not an excuse to drop out and wait; it is a call to dig in and work." *—Unknown Author*

~ 39 ~

Proverbs 19:18 – *"Discipline your son, for in that there is hope."*

Proverbs is a great book for practical ways to raise children. Some believe it to be extreme, as the author states in Proverbs 13:24, "He that spareth the rod hateth his child." Could this be advocating child abuse, some may ask? Taken in the total context of Proverbs, such an interpretation is absurd. In fact, those who do not discipline their children should be charged with child abuse. One of the worst forms of abuse is to permit a child to go undisciplined.

People have different methods of discipline. Some take away, some give, some spank, some give a time-out, some send to rooms, some speak firmly, while others scream. If we remember, the root word of discipline is "teach." It gives a totally new meaning to the word. Reread the Proverb now: "Teach your son, for in that there is hope." Whatever means we use to correct negative behavior or reinforce positive behavior, it should be a teaching process.

Being the last of seven children had its advantages for me. When I was growing up, my father was a very strict disciplinarian. Expressions like, "Do as I do, not as I say; a child should be seen and not heard; and speak only when spoken to" were commonplace affirmations in our home. Mother was a little more mellow but still carried a big stick. All this turned me off in my formative years. They were even tougher on my older brothers. It was commonplace for my dad to take off his belt and apply a quick lick to their back sides. I often watched their "correction" and decided to avoid the same at all costs.

In retrospect, I thank God for parents who cared enough to discipline. Without saying it in words, they gave me hope because of their concern for me. It often takes years and raising your own children before we can be so appreciative of love that sets limits. I have yet to meet a child or teenager who likes to be disciplined, however you define it. Many of the young people we have worked with at the Ranch had no concept of discipline. Or parents were very abusive in their discipline, which caused additional problems. But the writer of Proverbs gives us a great result: Discipline correctly administered can bring hope to the most disturbed child (remember, it's a teaching process).

> "Man needs, for his happiness, not only the enjoyment
> of this or that, but hope and enterprise and change."
> –*Bertrand Russell*

~ **40** ~

Proverbs 23:17–19 (NIV) – *"Do not let your heart envy sinners, but always be zealous for the fear of the Lord. There is surely a future hope for you, and your hope will not be cut off."*

The writer of this proverb speaks mainly of the future. Of course, there is always a danger we can be focused on where we will be instead of where we are. Consider these thoughts:

We convince ourselves that life will be better after we get married, have a baby, and then another. Then we are frustrated that the kids aren't old enough, and we'll be more content when they are.

After that, we're frustrated that we have teenagers to deal with. We will certainly be happy when they are out of that stage.

We tell ourselves that our life will be complete when our spouse gets his or her act together, when we get a nicer car, are able to go on a nice vacation, when we retire.

The truth is, there's no better time to be happy than right now. If not now, when?

Your life will always be filled with challenges. It's best to admit this to yourself and decide to be happy anyway.

A quote by Alfred D. Souza goes: "For a long time it had seemed to me that life was about to begin—real life. But there was always some obstacle in the way, something to be gotten through first, some unfinished business, time still to be served, a debt to be paid. Then life would begin. At last it dawned on me that these obstacles were MY LIFE."

This perspective has helped us to see that there is no way to happiness, except through our Lord Jesus Christ, that strengthens us.

A trip to the cardiologist can be stressful. In fact, a stress test can be very "stressful." Today we visit our spiritual cardiologist. We need help in developing a healthy spiritual heart, one that is not clogged with envy, evil thoughts, pride, using others, racism, sexual perversions (you fill in the blank), sin that could cause a major "heart attack." Scripture makes it clear that the heart is the command center for how we think, feel, and make choices. So we begin by AVOIDING any envy for sinners and developing a wholesome fear of the Lord. Then the Lord gives us hope for the present and future. Evil out —hope in—a healed heart for eternity. One author has called this "getting a real life."

So believe in Him, have faith in Him, and rely on Him every moment you have that He gives you to enjoy. And treasure it more because you have shared it with someone special. Special enough to spend your life with. And the family that He was so gracious to give you.

> "Life is a journey; ETERNITY is our destination. Make sure you spend that with Him."

~ **41** ~

Proverbs 26:12 (NKJV) – *"Do you see a man wise in his own eyes? There is more hope for a fool than for him."*

Conceit—a deadly sin. The author of Proverbs is referring to pride when he writes about "a man wise in his own eyes." There is an important line between being happy with the results we achieve and conceit over our success. The man in this proverb crossed the line and has less hope than a fool. Pretty strong language, but a great admonishment for all of us. This is a good time to do a pride check!

For many years I was involved in preaching renewal (revival) services in area churches. Attendance varied from church to church, as did response to RENEWAL (some places I felt there was a REVIVAL). One particular night I arrived at a church and found the parking lot packed with cars. For a moment the ego kicked in, and I was blessed to know they had come to hear me preach (a man wise in his own eyes). The Lord quickly brought me back down to earth when, upon entering the foyer of the church, a large sign with two arrows read: Wedding this Way and Revival this Way. The church was packed for the wedding—and a few showed up for the revival. So much for ego. Events like that help us from becoming a fool without hope.
Here are a few suggestions for AVOIDING the pitfalls of pride:

• Stay focused on the Lord!
• Remember the source of our ability and resources.
• Don't take yourself too seriously.
• When you receive praise, lift it up as an offering to God.

Reggie White, all-star football player for the Philadelphia Eagles and Green Bay Packers, offered this help when he spoke at a Ranch Hope Banquet. To paraphrase Reggie: "Since I was a teenager, I have received trophies and awards for football. I have a room filled with them. There was a time when I received so many of them it pumped me up with pride. High school, college, and then pros all recognized my exploits on the gridiron. But I have decided that since I know the Lord, they are all to HIS glory, and one day I will cast them all at Jesus' feet." That is great advice from a man who died in the prime of his life. Reggie had much more hope than a fool who played on an ego trip.

The writer of Proverbs (many believe it to be Solomon) had his own problems with conceit. As he was blessed in his life with more and more material blessings, he began a downward spiral. We see this very often in every field of endeavor: politics, sports, economics, and, of course, even in the church. Today we can look for examples of people who have risen above the ego and are focused on our Lord, who provides every blessing, material and spiritual.

"In our desert of grief, Jesus can provide an oasis of hope." *–Bill Crowder*

~ 42 ~

Proverbs 29:20 (NKJV) – *"Do you see a man hasty in his words? There is more hope for a fool than for him."*

The author of these words is focusing on anger or a bad temper. Some people have struggled with controlling their temper since childhood. A temper tantrum can be thrown by children and adults acting like children. My mother used to remind me of a proverb: "Haste maketh waste," and then she would add, "Make sure your mind is in gear before you run your mouth." Others have said it more eloquently, like James who wrote, "Let every man be swift to hear, slow to speak." The writer of Ecclesiastes preceded James with this thought, "A talkative man is dangerous in his city, and he that is rash in his words shall be hated." Hope is not based on being a fast talker; it is definitely not based on losing our temper.

This can be illustrated with a story. A boy named Harry arrived at our boys' ranch. He was an attractive child—tall and lanky and with a sense of humor. He often was characterized as a cross between a comedian and a chimpanzee. One of his attributes was a concern for using big words. He loved to impress people with big words, but he had no vocabulary. He loved to talk and was never at a loss for words.

One week in devotions, we studied a verse in the 23rd Psalm: "The Lord is my shepherd, I shall not want, He maketh me to lie down in green pastures." Harry asked to lead in prayer. This was unusual for him, and we were nervous about giving him such an opportunity. But he started on track, "Lord, please be my shepherd; keep me on the straight and narrow path." But then came the bomb, "Please help us boys get pasteurized."

Harry had the right idea, but his words were spoken in haste, and most of us had to break up laughing after the AMEN. Of course, he gave new meaning to being "pasteurized." Years later, Harry called me. I was stunned as he told me of the premature death of his wife. His early education in the 23rd Psalm helped him through this tragedy. I shared with him that we are confronted with the shadow of death. It is only a shadow, and we will get through that valley. Harry made an error of interpretation as a teenager. But those of us who are maturing in the faith will find hope in avoiding the actions of a "fool."

"True hope focuses not on plans and prescriptions but on the person of God." *–Susan Lenzkes*

~ 43 ~

Ecclesiastes 9:4 (KJV) – *"For to him that is joined to all the living, there is hope: for a living dog is better than a dead lion."*

As long as we're alive, there is some hope. An old cliché states, "Hope springs eternal in the human breast." A character named Bailey sings in Festus, "All have hopes, how wretched they may be, or blessed, it is hope which lifts the lark so high, hope for a lighter air and bluer sky." In this verse, however, there is a strange transition. The verse uses an analogy of a living dog and a dead lion. In ancient Palestine, dogs were not pets or considered man's best friend. In fact, they were despised and considered loathsome. On the other hand, the lion was nobility, regarded as powerful and great. This proverb, therefore, in common use, is interpreted to mean that even the vilest creature living is better than the best dead. In the context of these books of the Bible and the times in which it was written, there is an important message.

As we grow older, we need a message repeated again that we

learned as children in Sunday school; however, we need the senior version. Read or sing along these inspirational words.

> Jesus loves me, this I know,
> Though my hair is white as snow
> Though my sight is growing dim,
> Still he bids me trust in Him.
> (CHORUS)
> YES, JESUS LOVES ME. YES, JESUS LOVES ME.
> YES, JESUS LOVES ME, FOR THE BIBLE TELLS
> ME SO.

Though my steps are oh, so slow,
With my hand in His I'll go
On through life, let come what may
He'll be there to lead the way.

When nights are dark and long,
In my heart He puts a song.
Telling me in words so clear,
"Have no fear, for I am near."

When my work on earth is done,
And life's victories have been won
He will take me home above,
Then I'll understand His love.

I love Jesus, does he know?
Have I ever told Him so?
Jesus loves to hear me say,
That I love Him every day.

Make the best use of our lives, knowing Jesus loves us with the changing years. With Jesus we are joined to the living hope. We become "living lions," not dead dogs. Do all we can to help all we can, in every way we can because death is inevitable. While we are living, we contribute to life. At death, contributions are limited to what people remember. A quote from an old pastor still makes sense: "Do your giving while you're living, so you knowing where it's going."

> "Don't expect the worse . . . expect God." (That is real hope.) *–Lloyd Ogilvie*

~ **44** ~

Isaiah 38:18 (KJV) – *"For the grave cannot praise thee, death can not celebrate thee: they that go down into the pit cannot hope for thy truth."*

Hezekiah has been a good king of Israel. He has served the Lord all his life, but now he is very ill (probably the result of an infected boil or ulcer). Keep in mind, at this time in Israel a long life was the sign of God's favor. For Hezekiah to die in the prime of life would be the sign of God's judgment. Is it any wonder that Hezekiah, as he deals with his illness and possible death, writes about the negative aspects of his infirmity?

Remember, the book of Isaiah was written in BC (before Christ). The prophet Isaiah has paid a visit to Hezekiah and tells him "to get his house in order." Hezekiah is now facing death. As king, he is also facing an enemy in the nation of Assyria. The Assyrians are threatening to invade Israel and capture its people. All this has made him "lose heart and become depressed." The king prays and repents in grief. Amazingly enough (and only God knows why), he is given fifteen more years to live. Today, however, we are concentrating on his thoughts of death and dying. Hezekiah believes we can only praise God while we are on earth. We cannot celebrate when we're dead; there is no hope.

As Christians, we live on this side of the empty tomb (remember when we used to write AD). Praise God for the empty tomb. Praise God for Resurrection Sunday (Easter). My mind goes back to a Sunday I was preaching in our chapel during Lent. Facing sixty hyperactive young men, I wanted to convey the truth about eternal life. A friend had given me a wonderful, easy-to-understand analogy for the Christian's understanding of death.

A small boy was riding in a pickup truck with his father. It was a warm July afternoon, and they had the windows down. Suddenly, a small honeybee flew into the cab. The little boy screamed, "Get him, Daddy; get him!" You see, the boy was allergic to the sting of a bee. He had once spent time in the hospital from an allergic reaction. His father was well aware of this and quickly grabbed the bee but then released it. "Daddy, you missed him," he cried. But the father pulled off the road and showed his son what he had done. "Look, honey; look at Daddy's finger. There's the stinger. The bee won't hurt you. I've taken the bee's stinger."

Paul asked the church later in one of his letters (1 Cor. 15:55): "O death where is thy victory, oh grave where is thy sting?" He knew the answer: Jesus had taken the sting out of death. Paul writes, "Thanks be to God! He gives us the victory through our Lord Jesus Christ." The boys that Sunday morning had gotten the message, as I hope each of us has as we lose loved ones and confront our own death. When we get down to the grave, we have hope of still praising God.

When we meditate on the word guidance, I kept seeing "dance" at the end of the word. I remember reading that doing God's will is a lot like dancing. When two people try to lead, nothing feels right. The movement doesn't flow with the music, and everything is quite uncomfortable and jerky. When one person realizes that, and lets the other lead, both bodies begin to flow with the music. One gives gentle cues, perhaps with a nudge to the back or by pressing lightly in one direction or another. It's as if two become one body, moving beautifully. The dance takes surrender, willingness, and attentiveness from one person and gentle guidance and skill from the other.

My eyes drew back to the word guidance. When I saw "G," I thought of God, followed by "U" and "I." "God, "U," and "I" dance. God, you and I dance. As I lowered my head, I became willing to trust that I would get guidance about my life. Once again, I became willing to let God lead.

My prayer for you today is that God's blessings and mercies be upon you on this day and every day. May you abide in God as God abides in you. Dance together with God, trusting God to lead and to guide you through each season of your life. And I hope you dance!

> "Hope is not finding strength to go on; it is going on when you don't have strength." *–Anonymous*

~ 45 ~

Isaiah 57:10 – *"You were wearied with the length of your way, but you did not say, "It is hopeless"; you found new life for your strength, and so you were not faint."*

My hope hath removed like a tree (torn up like a tree). Most of us hope to live a life of tranquility. When we are younger, we think of a good job, a loving spouse, children, a nice home, and the routine pleasure of family and friends. Job had all this, and then the calamities set in. Is it any wonder he felt hope had been torn up like a tree?

From the book *Hope for the Troubled Heart,* a story was told about Billy Graham's wife, Ruth. She had a terrible fall and suffered a concussion. Ruth was unconscious for nearly a week; she broke her foot in five places, broke a rib, cracked a vertebra, and injured her hip. Some of those injuries lingered with her for many years. But when she initially regained consciousness after a week, Billy Graham writes in his book that he found his wife had lost a great deal of her memory. Most disturbing to Ruth Graham was that she had forgotten all Scriptures she had been learning throughout the years. The verses of a lifetime were more precious to her than any of her material possessions, and now she couldn't bring them back from memory.

One night Ruth Graham was praying, and she said, "Lord, take anything I have, but please bring back the Bible verses." Ruth Graham says it was almost immediately that a verse came to mind. "I have loved Thee with an everlasting love, therefore with loving kindness have I drawn Thee." Strangely, Ruth Graham did not remember at that point ever memorizing that verse, but she believes that the Lord brought it back to her. She continued after this to memorize. She found that as she got older, it took longer. More and more she was able to put longer and longer parts of the Bible into her memory. Why? Because she always believed that you should take Scriptures, memorize them, and put them in your heart and mind so when you need them during times of adversity, during times of difficulty, the Scriptures can give you hope and strength. I too recommend that today, hide the word of God in your heart so that in times of need you can recall those verses of Scripture to memory.

Maybe today you are living with or facing circumstances like Job or Ruth Graham. Trees and dreams do get uprooted. But we must remember they are still only trees. I miss the old farm-house where we started, but it was just a farmhouse. We have planted other trees; we have built many buildings. Job lost much, but we know the end of the story that God replaced everything and even gave him a new family. When trees are torn down, plant new ones; when dreams are shattered, dream new dreams. That's what hope is all about.

"My hopes are not always realized, but I always hope."
–Ovid

~ 46 ~

Jeremiah 2:25 – *"Don't run bare foot and thirsty! You say, "There is no hope" for I have loved strangers (aliens) and after them will I go."*

Jeremiah was a young prophet. He was set aside from the time of his birth to serve the Lord and also was known as a priest. He actually prophesied during the reign of five kings and was part of a great deal of Israel's history.

In today's verse, Jeremiah gives advice from God to Israel. Don't wear yourselves out physically chasing after the evils of your culture. Like many times in the past, Israel continued to worship idols that would disappoint them and leave them hope-less. They had to focus on the positive possibility of hope.

A number of years ago, the Washington Redskins football team pulled it off. They had a football team made up of castoffs, kind of a ragtag group of castoffs. Most of them were considered beyond their prime. But along came a dynamic coach, George Allen. That Washington coach decided to take them, although they were old, some considered over the hill, and he began to turn them into a championship team. The long of it is—this group of gray-bearded athletes had a great season because George Allen gave them hope in themselves and in each other. They put together a winner.

We have a notion in our country that is crazy. Somehow, magically, when someone turns fifty-five or sixty-five or seventy, that person should retire. Notice it shouldn't be fifty-six or sixty-four or sixty-nine—no, the magic numbers are fifty-five, sixty-five, or seventy. Of course, you would think that magically on one of those birthdays you are struck by a wand of a gray haired, wrinkled fairy and become old. The longer I live, the more I see that age comes upon us when our mind tells us we are getting old. A good friend told me not long ago that he became depressed when he turned forty, and it took him a couple weeks to adjust to it. I have another friend who turned fifty and went through the same problem. Sometimes this occurs because people wear themselves out running after the wrong pursuits.

The Bible tells us we have three score and ten years. That's a full life, but today many people live productive lives beyond that. Today I would like you to say, "Lord, whatever time you have given me, I want to be grateful for it, and I want to use the rest of my days as best I can. I don't want to have someone think I am over the hill. Like those football players, I want to still believe in myself and believe in You and believe that I can accomplish things even when others think I am over the hill. I want to run barefoot after the Lord and drink in the living waters." And stay away from those aliens.

"Hope in anything except God makes our hope depend on circumstances; basing our hope in God means we find hope where it didn't seem to exist." *–Kristen Escovedo*

~ 47 ~

Jeremiah 3:23 (KJV) – *"Truly in vain is salvation hoped for from the hills, and from the multitude of mountains: truly in the LORD our God is the salvation of Israel."*

In our mind's eye we can think of beautiful mountains. I have seen the Western Rockies, Canadian Rockies, Appalachians, the Alps, and many other spectacular ranges. Israel also was a place of beautiful hills and mountains. We automatically think of Mount Sinai and Moses receiving the Ten Commandments. The psalmist wrote the familiar words, "I will lift up my eyes unto the hills." Jeremiah, as a young prophet, served God in a difficult time. He spoke of mountains and hills in a negative sense; some listened, but many rejected his message.

Tragically, the mountains and hills became the focal points for idol worship. Israel had to once again learn in the present as they had in the past that the godly life does not come from images or related sex orgies. The nation was ruined time and again by vain and shameful worship that included eating, drinking, partying, and even at times human sacrifice. Salvation hoped for came from a different style and focus. Sacrifices of animals and humans were commonplace, and the people thought they were appeasing these gods.

Jonathan Wilson-Hartgrove (a modern Jeremiah) has written a book, The Awakening of Hope. He writes of how God moves in human history, sometimes bringing light to people in darkness (idol worship). Like a flash, God gives a picture of hope. Then the pictures of hope are kept in a photo album. We can refer to that album and remember the places, people, and times where hope emerged. Jonathan encourages us not to start with frustration or disappointment, but rather places where hope emerges. "Start with Israel in Egypt, shepherds near Bethlehem, people breaking bread in Emmaus, monks in a desert, people off the radar of history where hope is stirring."

"Truly in the Lord is the salvation of Israel." Can we really say it any better than that? Suppose we take the word Israel and put in America! Or better yet, let's not think of a nation, let's think on a personal level and put in our name. Today would be a great day to remember that we must be saved from the "vain world's golden store, from each idol that would keep us saying, 'Christian, love me more.'" These words come from the old gospel hymn "Jesus Calls Us." Having sung that so often as a child and young adult, I began to realize that the message of the music is for each of us. I can remember so many idols that kept me—movie stars, entertainers, sports celebrities, political leaders, business personalities, all successful in their own way, but human, frail, and limited. Like hope from the hills, they have perished, and every day I am blessed that I turned from those idols to hope in Jesus.

> "O God, we come to you today empty, fill us with hope,
> a hope that never falters because it is rooted in your con-
> stancy." –*Prayer of Rev. Tom Fisher*

~ 48 ~

Jeremiah 14:8 (NKJV) – "O the Hope of Israel, his Savior in time of trouble."

Drought is a challenge for any people, especially a culture living in Jeremiah's time. In this case, drought is a judgment upon the backsliding people of Judah. Often in Scripture we read how God used periods of drought to bring people to their knees. In fact, God had warned Israel a number of times that such natural calamities could be visited upon them if they sinned against Him. The picture painted by Jeremiah describes a culture of adulteries, prostitution, and often abominations (acts such as idolatry and other immorality). It is not a pretty picture of people who have been chosen of God. Because of sin, the people are suffering from lack of water, and Jeremiah writes about even the nobility looks for water and finds only empty cisterns. Animals roam about and find only cracked earth. It is a time of national calamity that needs hope, and that hope is to come from the Eternal God. Jeremiah prays to God to act not according to what the people deserved, but according to the fact He is their Savior.

Every nation has known some form of drought. Here in America we have witnessed the cycles of nature have devastating effects on different parts of our country at different times. However, the most "devastating" type of drought to hit any people is spiritual calamities caused by people turning away from God. Billy Graham, in his often-quoted prayer, sums it up for us here in America:

> "Heavenly Father, we come before you today to ask your forgiveness and to seek your direction and guidance. We

know Your Word says, 'Woe to those who call evil good,' but that is exactly what we have done. We have lost our spiritual equilibrium and reversed our values. We have exploited the poor and called it the lottery. We have rewarded laziness and called it welfare. We have killed our unborn and called it choice. We have shot abortionists and called it justifiable. We have neglected to discipline our children and called it building self-esteem. We have abused power and called it politics. We have coveted our neighbor's possessions and called it ambition. We have polluted the air with profanity and pornography and called it freedom of expression. We have ridiculed the time-honored values of our forefathers and called it enlightenment. Search us, O God, and know our hearts today; cleanse us from every sin and set us free. Amen!"

The good news is that Judah and America have a Savior who is our hope in time of trouble. In verse 9 we read, "Yet thou, O Lord, art in the midst of us and we are called by thy name, leave us not." For the people of Judah it was too late, but not for us. Judgment had begun for them. Two thousand six hundred years later, we read these words and know that the Savior Jesus has come and died to save us from sins as a nation, a church, and an individual. Jesus often used the metaphor of being the living water. Water is always the best solution to drought. It's time to repent and find hope today at the cross, where all sin was dealt with.

"When you reach rock bottom, hope comes by placing your feet on the Rock, Christ Jesus!" *—Anonymous*

~ **49** ~

Jeremiah 14:22–23 (NIV) – *"Do any of the worthless idols of the nations bring rain? Do skies themselves send down showers? No, it is you, Lord our God. Therefore our hope is in you, for you are the one who does all this."*

Worthless idols—now where do we begin? From Jeremiah's perspective, the Gentiles had their idols, and the prophet mockingly asks, "Can the idols cause rain?" Every generation of man has had their idols, including the Jews of Jeremiah's time—worthless idols—no value whatsoever. Of course, for those that believed in idols, they would argue their value. There was a whole industry dependent upon idol worship. But the obvious answer to Jeremiah's question is No! God made the heavens and the earth and all that is—that is an affirmation of faith we need to hear loud and clear. Without that belief, our hope is meaningless.

I define an idol as "anything less than God that is the center of our worship." We can worship people, things, nature, philosophies, government, ourselves, and the list goes on and on. As I once mentioned, worth ship comes from an old English word worship—that which is highest worth to us —we worship. It reminds me of a short science fiction story I read as a teenager. It may have been written by Ray Bradbury and is so applicable to this study.

Atomic wars had decimated our planet. Our major cities, plants, and institutions lay in ruin. Here and there are bands of people trying to find food and shelter just to exist. The story centers on one group that roams New York City and finds people living in a bombed-out apartment house. This group is all huddled together praying—praying to their gods that existed before the war. To the amazement of the visiting group, they find the worshippers kneeling before radios, stereos, TV sets, automatic washers, and other appliances—all their "gods" before the atomic holocaust. The message of the sci-fi story was evident! Idols created by technology had replaced the living God. (Today could we include computers, iPods, and the many new hi-tech deities!)

Our hope is in God, creator and sustainer of this universe. Anything less than God is an idol. You would think that His creatures would understand this. God is CREATOR; man is CREATED. The Apostles' Creed still gives us a firm foundation for hope: "I believe in God the Father Almighty, maker of heaven and earth. Amen!

"It's not what we gather, but what we scatter that brings hope to a troubled world." *—Anonymous*

~ 50 ~

Jeremiah 17:7(KJV) – *"Blessed is the man that trusteth in the Lord, and whose hope the Lord is."*

Want to be blessed? Trust in the Lord and hope in the Lord. A one-two punch for every believer. Jeremiah echoes the word of the Lord as he contrasts the person who trusts in man and departs from the Lord with those who are blessed. It is a no-brainer. To be blessed today, to be happy, to be envied—trust and hope in the Lord. It is a formula that does not fail.

Jeremiah then uses an often-quoted illustration. The believer shall "be like a tree planted by the waters, and spreads out its roots by the river; it does not fear when the heat comes, the leaves will be green, and will not have problems during the drought, but will continue to grow fruit." Wow! Does that say it all? A person who has no trust or hope will experience just the opposite—their roots will find no water, they will have fear during the time of heat, their leaves will wither, a drought will cause anxiety, and they will bear no fruit. Now which course shall we choose?

One night I was preaching at a church in our area and was blessed by a Gospel song new to me. It was called "Jesus on the Main Line." The song encouraged us to call Him up, tell Him what you want! If you want to be blessed, call Him up!

Our source of blessing, prayer, communication is with the Lord. It is an interesting comparison, but we know heaven provides a much better service. Someone has written this humorous (yet insightful) illustration:

Call Him Up
God doesn't have an unlisted number. He excludes no one and gives priority to the "poor in spirit." He wants you to call.

It's a local call. God is omnipresent. You don't have to select AT&T, Sprint, T-Mobile, Verizon, or any other company. One of His names, Jehovah-Shammah, means "the God who is (always) there."

It's person-to-person. You don't even have to talk to a secretary, who asks, "May I ask who is calling?" He has your number.

You are never put on hold. You do not hear a nice voice say every thirty seconds, "You are important to us. Our lines are busy. Your call will be answered in the order in which it was received." He is able to converse with millions at the same time.

God doesn't have an answering machine. You won't hear a canned message: "Sorry, I can't come to the phone just now. At the sound of the tone, leave a massage and phone number. I'll get back to you as soon as I can."

He doesn't work a five-day week. He's available every day. He doesn't have a nine-to-five job. He's there 24 hours a day, 365 days a year.

You don't have to worry about language barriers. He started the barriers at the Tower of Babel (Genesis 11:9). He understands all of the more than 2,700 languages or dialects spoken around the world. He has a universal language called "love," and it has no hard-to-understand accent.

You can call from anywhere. You don't need a cellular phone in your car or even a satellite hookup. You don't need a World Wide Web address; just talk and He'll answer.

There's no charge. There's no monthly bill. His Son has already paid the price-a gift that lasts forever.

By the way, He's by the throne phone right now waiting to hear from you. Don't wait (as some do) till you need to call 911.

"I have more hope in an army of 100 sheep led by a lion, than an army of 100 lions led by a sheep." *–Edited quote of Talleyrand*

~ 51 ~

Jeremiah 17:13 (KJV) – *"O Lord, the hope of Israel, all that forsake thee shall be ashamed, and they that depart from me shall be written in the earth [instead of heaven]."*

Jeremiah has been called the weeping prophet, but he has also been called the prophet of the "new covenant" (new contract). Hope for Israel was to come through a new covenant with the Lord. It always amazes me when Hollywood stars, athletes, labor unions, or school teachers negotiate new contracts. The process is often long and arduous. The sides see each other as adversaries, instead of working for a common good. One summer I worked for a Chrysler tank plant. It was a summer job that lasted three months, but two weeks were spent on strike. A fellow college student and I figured that the employees gained 15 cents an hour, and it would take ten years to make up what they lost in wages for two weeks. I saw firsthand how divisive and contentious contract negotiations can be.

But Jeremiah represents the Lord and foretells a great new covenant (contract) for his people (without negotiation). Remember, he lists their sins—eight of them. Let's review so we can see the significance of the new covenant. Israel had forsaken God, questioned the word of God, persecuted the prophets, abused the Sabbath, refused to obey God, no longer listened to God, did not follow His instructions, and were stiff necked (conceited). No wonder a new contract was needed. The Jews had definitely broken the original.

So the good news is a Messiah will save Israel and Judah from sins by shedding His blood in the new covenant. We are talking about major changes in God's dealing with the human condition. No wonder Jeremiah prophesies, "All who forsake the Lord shall be written in the earth, instead of heaven." Now you don't have to be a rocket scientist to know we need the new covenant, a Messiah, for our hope. We want our names written in heaven (later called the Lamb's Book of Life), not just in some ledger here on earth.

Today's verse is a part of Jeremiah's prayer, beginning with, "O Lord, the hope of Israel." We could stop right there and be blessed. Keep in mind that Jeremiah's prophecy is by word count the longest in the Bible (remember that trivia if you are on Jeopardy on TV). The first twenty-nine chapters are full of judgment, but by the time we reach chapter 30, Jeremiah is offering hope, but today we get our first glimpse of that message. Jeremiah's prayer has the starting point of hope in the Lord. When we are in a nation, a culture, a race of people that are at odds with God's covenant, remember they are hopeless. No expectation of success. It is our calling to be a Jeremiah to our generation.

> Prayer: "Lord, help me mourn those things that break your heart. I need to be a bearer of hope in the midst of so much despair." *–Scripture Union Devotional*

~ **52** ~

Jeremiah 17:17 (KJV) – *"Thou art my hope in the day of evil."*

Jeremiah lived in a day of evil. Surrounded by evil prophets, evil people, and evil leaders, he was called to warn his generation of the coming judgment. But most people did not listen and continued on their way to destruction. Sound familiar? Human history is filled with story after sad story of those who chose evil and ignored warnings from God's messengers. Though Jeremiah struggled with many difficulties, including persecution and even loneliness, he continually sought God in prayer, his source of hope. Chapter 17 contains one such prayer. Talk about a prayer from the heart! Jeremiah is up-front and frank with God. Note these words as he begins the prayer: "Heal me, O Lord! Save me, O Lord!"

Short and to the point. He then brings his critical remarks directly to the Lord. They say to me, "Where is this judgment you talk about? Let it come now." Jeremiah believes they are taunting him, mocking his message. This is upsetting to the prophet because he does not take pleasure in warning people. At heart he was still a shepherd and was concerned for people's welfare. Every preacher, prophet and pastor, judge, and lover of his flock has faced this dilemma.

As the prayer continues, we arrive at verse 17. "Do not be a terror to me, you are my hope in the day of evil." Strange use of the word terror, but it shows Jeremiah's condition at this time and why he needs to pray. It is similar to Peter when Jesus calls him to walk on the water. Peter begins to sink, and he gives the shortest prayer in the Bible—"SAVE ME!" I think all of us have been there. Peter's help came when he got his eyes back on Jesus. For Jeremiah, the terror may have been physical, mental, or emotional, but it was real, and he needed HOPE.

Interestingly enough, hope in this case would be best translated refuge or shelter. Wow! Jeremiah knows he needs a place of safety and security in the face of all the danger and hopelessness he is facing: Don't miss this exciting spiritual blessing! The world around us is ignoring God, His love, and His law, like a vehicle out of control speeding off a cliff, but God gives the believer a place of refuge and shelter.

If you can sing, sing these words of the old hymn. (If you can't carry a tune, recite them aloud.)

> The Lord's our rock; in Him we hide.
> A shelter in the time of storm.
> Content whatever ill betide.
> A shelter in the time of storm.
> O Jesus is a rock in a weary land.
> A weary land, a weary land.
> O Jesus is my Rock in a weary land.
> A shelter in the time of storm.

"If sin rules in me, God's life in me will be killed; if God rules in me, sin in me will be killed." *—Oswald Chambers*

~ 53 ~

Jeremiah 18:12 (KJV) – *"And they said, There is no hope: but we will walk after our own devices [plans] [follow our evil imaginations]."*

Jeremiah saw his nation Judah falling apart. Like many nations since then, the initial problem was decay from within. The Jews had lost their moral compass and were walking after their own devices. One modern translation makes it very clear for us with the phrase "following their own evil imaginations." However, to make matters worse, Jeremiah's people were also under constant duress from their enemies. Military powers opposed to them wanted to see the destruction of Judah. The warnings of this great prophet went unheeded as Judah slipped further and further into spiritual chaos.

Recently I saw a program on television that talked about people who lose particular senses. They may lose the sense of hearing or touch or smell or taste. It amazed me that there can be certain diseases that take over the body, that take over a person's ability to smell or taste. One of the other people on the program had lost the ability to feel pain. Can you imagine what that would be like? Especially if you injured yourself and there was no pain?

Whenever I am in my morning devotions, I thank God for some of those areas of life I forget to thank Him for each day. For the basic senses, I thank the Lord that I can even sit at my desk with my head bowed and be able to communicate with Him mentally, to be able to think, to be able to open my eyes in a few seconds, and to be able to see. To taste the morning breakfast, to smell the coffee getting cooked, to be able to just accept the gifts that very often I take for granted. After seeing the people on television, I fully appreciate the value of senses.

Helen Steiner Rice wrote these words, a fitting way to close these thoughts today, "Thank you, thank you God for little things that often come our way. The things we take for granted and don't mention when we pray. The unexpected courtesy, the thoughtful kindly deed. A hand reached out to help us in a time of sudden need. O make us more aware, Dear God, of little daily graces, that come to us with sweet surprise from never dreamed of places."

Those that walk after their own plans have lost the most important sense—the spiritual. God warned the people of Judah through Jeremiah, but they were convinced there was no hope. Hopelessness usually follows godlessness. Let us be sensible people of God today and avoid the trap of following our own devices.

"Lord, save us all from a hope tree that has lost the faculty of putting out blossoms." *—Mark Twain*

~ 54 ~

Jeremiah 31:17 (KJV) – *"And there is hope in thine end, saith the Lord, that thy children shall come again to their own border."*

In this study, Jeremiah borrows from Israel's history. He focuses on the experience of Rachel, Jacob's wife. Emphasis is placed upon her sorrows. Every parent sometime or other is concerned about the future of his or her children. In Rachel's case it led to uncontrollable weeping. She was the biological mother to Benjamin, Manasseh, and Ephraim. Some believe she is the spiritual mother of the whole of Israel. Rachel had wanted children all her life and died in childbirth when Benjamin was born. His original name was to be "Son of Sorrow" (Benoni). Jeremiah uses this analogy to show that sorrow would come to the nation of Israel. We are blessed today looking at verse 17 to know that hope comes even in the midst of weeping. The women of Israel would weep for their children, but there will be restoration of the nation under the Messiah. Captivity will be short lived.

The files of Ranch Hope are filled with the stories of weeping parents, parents concerned about the future of their children. Often our ministry to these young people is their final hope before detention center, or worse—prison. One parent stands out in my mind. She had recently received Christ as her Savior and was trying to rebuild her family. After divorcing an abusive husband, she married a man who was supportive of her spiritual concerns. But her two sons were in total rebellion. They didn't like the new father or the changed mother. It was great the old way—no dad at home, mom all messed up, and the boys ruling the roost. But now the stepdad and mom were religious freaks. As troubled teens, the new life for their mother was hell for them.

After problems in the community and at school, the oldest son came to the Ranch. He was a handful. The family's problems became our problems. We would find him using marijuana, sniffing glue, fighting, acting out in school. All classic characteristics of a troubled child. On visiting Sundays, the mother and stepfather would often leave in tears. Can you imagine how difficult it was to help them be "hopeful"? To further complicate the problem, the mother was struck with cancer. It was her daily prayer that this rebellious son would change before her death. These words from the book of Jeremiah would have been a great comfort to her: "THERE IS HOPE IN THINE END, SAITH THE LORD. THY CHILDREN SHOULD BE RESTORED."

Jesus spoke of many prodigals. His most famous parable of the prodigal son is the story of this young man. I preached a sermon on Mother's Day in our Ranch Chapel. That message helped change the boy's heart before his mother's death. He often said to me that he loved his mother and was sorry for the way he treated her. But he never showed this in his relationship with her. That Sunday our Lord changed him forever. Like the prodigal in Jesus' parable, he came back to where he should be in life. His mother's weeping was turned to joy before she went to be with the Lord. Today you may struggle with a troubled child, grandchild, or other member of a family going through such a struggle. Share this passage of Scripture with them. Encourage them to HOPE!

> "The future belongs to those who give the next generation reason for hope." *—Pierre Teilhard de Chardin*

~ 55 ~

Jeremiah 50:7 (KJV) – *"All that found them have devoured them: and their adversaries said, We offend not, because they have sinned against the Lord, the habitation of justice, even the Lord, the hope of their fathers."*

God had used the Babylonians to chasten Israel. The Hebrew

people had not kept the covenant established with their fathers. Thus, they had been scattered as a people. Babylon had been invaded by the Medo-Persian empire, and God wanted His people out of that nation before it was destroyed. However, as they leave and the process of regathering begins, they still suffer much at the hand of their adversaries, all because they neglected the "hope of their fathers."

Today that can also be a problem. How do we pass it on? Jeremiah recognized the fact that his generation had the responsibility to pass the truth of God onto the next generation. Have you ever gone into a church and been overwhelmed by the small attendance? A writer said that we are just one generation from extinction. We might consider the following story and be inspired.

One of the great hymns of the church is "Faith of our Fathers." This faith has brought hope to many of us as we remember our rich history. Yet, we also know there is a strong tendency with each generation to forget the lessons of the past. A common saying is, "History teaches us that history teaches us nothing." Generation after generation seems to make the same mistake, committing the same sins. We have a tendency to forget the faith and the hope of our fathers. Our faith is rooted in history.

Frederick Faber, author of the hymn, lived during the nineteenth century (1814–1863). As an Anglican minister, he felt the new religious movements of his day were dangerous. Believers had begun to put too much emphasis upon personal experience and were losing their roots with the past. Thus he left the Anglican ministry and became a Roman Catholic. For him, the Catholic church had maintained its relationship with the past. Still, he missed the hymns he had enjoyed in the past. Thus he wrote hymns to fill the spiritual void. "Faith of our Fathers" is one such hymn. Review these words today and make them a prayer and point of meditation.

"Faith of our Fathers! Living still. In spite of dungeon, fire, and sword. O how our hearts beat high with joy, Whene'er we hear that glorious word. Faith of our Fathers, holy faith! We will be true to thee till death."

"To live without hope is to cease to live." –*Fyodor Dostoyevsky*

~ 56 ~

Lamentations 3:18 (KJV) – *"And I said, My strength and my hope is perished from the Lord."*

All of us that have experienced a loss can relate to Lamentations. Jerusalem fell to Babylon in 586 BC. Crushed by the fall of his homeland, Jeremiah writes a series of poems. Lamentations is composed of five poems. This third chapter contains the longest with sixty-six verses, written by Jeremiah, called the weeping prophet. The Jews had been taken captive and Jerusalem destroyed. Thus the poetry expresses the concerns and suffering of the people during this horrendous period. Like any time of captivity, there was a great amount of unbelief, and people seemed to receive no message from the Lord. Jeremiah was frustrated over Jerusalem's decline, just as we grow concerned when we see signs of our nation's decline.

Today's verse must be understood as the lowest point in

Jeremiah's writing. Can he put it any more bluntly than to write, "My strength and my hope is perished from Jehovah"? Everything had caught up to him. What was to this point in the poetry an oblique reference now becomes the focal point— Jehovah has deserted him, and Jeremiah is in despair. Yet we can find hope in despair as we repent (change course) and pray for revival.

If we are honest, we, too, can relate events that have caused such despair. My good friend, Dot Worth, an excellent Bible teacher and host of the "Women Alive" radio broadcast, said such a condition can cause us to become either bitter or better. The child of God wants to become better, not bitter. Little did Dot realize when she said that, she would be put to such a test. Just before preaching at a Good Friday prayer breakfast, Dot suffered a debilitating stroke. For months she was unable to minister the Word as a teacher and was confined to a wheelchair. In addition to this, her husband Phil was also dealing with physical disabilities and soon passed away. Dot struggled back, and after nearly two years of "captivity," suffering, and despair, she began to teach from her wheelchair. The history of the church is filled with those who chose to get better, not bitter. Today, make the right choice! Consider this provocative essay:

When God wants to drill a man and thrill a man and skill a man
When God wants to mold a man to plan the noblest part!
When He yearns with all His heart to create so bold and great a man
That all the world shall be amazed,
WATCH God's Methods; Watch God's way.

How God ruthlessly perfects whom He royally elects!
How He hammers and bends Him, and with mighty blows
Converts him into trial shapes of clay which only God understands;
So our tortured heart may be crying, and we lift questioning hands!
How he bends but never breaks when our good He undertakes
How he uses whom He chooses and with every purpose fuses him,
By every act induces him to try His splendor out.
GOD KNOW'S WHAT HE'S ABOUT.

"Everything that is done in the world is done by hope."
–Martin Luther

~ 57 ~

Lamentations 3:21 (KJV) – *"This I recall to my mind, therefore have I hope."*

Finally, a ray of light. Jeremiah had been in the "pits" and needed a revival. Revival is needed in the church, the nation, and in our personal lives. By definition it means "life again" (*re-viva*). If Jeremiah knew distress and despondency, he also knew that a child of God could not stay in that position. It was a time for revival. Hope enters.

Notice that hope for Jeremiah started with his memory and humility. He remembered the Lord and humbled himself before

Him. All that was in this great prophet bowed before the Eternal God, and he realized he was the creature and God the Creator. This is a starting place for revival. New life can begin in anyone who reaches this point.

Years ago I preached a sermon entitled "Churchianity vs. Christianity" as a youth pastor filling in for the senior pastor, Rev. Bob Acheson. I thought it was one of my better messages. A local businessman visited our church where I was assistant minister. My ego blossomed as the visitor congratulated me on a powerful sermon. In my heart I knew he had come to hear me.

Months later I was invited to preach at his church as a guest speaker. Much to my amazement, on the way out of the morning worship service, the businessman stopped, shook my hand, and said, "You know I visited your church this summer. Tell Brother Acheson I can still remember that sermon he preached, 'Christianity vs. Churchianity.' It was powerful!" What? Hello! That was me—that was my sermon! God had a message for me that morning: Stay humble before Him; don't care who gets the credit. Why? So you can stay focused on the real source of hope.

Do you need "revival" today? Do you need to believe that God is a God of hope? Have there been circumstances that have you lamenting like the weeping prophet Jeremiah? Our hope is based upon remembering who God is and who we are. "This I recall to mind, therefore I have hope." Think on these things:

LIVE each day to the fullest.
GET the most from each hour, each day,
and each age of life.
Then you can look forward with confidence

and back without regrets.

And don't be afraid to be happy.

ENJOY what is beautiful.

LOVE with all your heart and soul.

LEARN to forgive yourself for your faults, for this is the first step in learning to forgive others—and to have a renewed spirit.

DISREGARD what the world owes you, and concentrate on what you owe the world.

No matter how troublesome the cares of life may seem to you at times, this is still a beautiful world.

ACT as if everything depended upon you, and

PRAY as if everything depended upon God.

"A strong mind always hopes, and always has cause to hope." *–Thomas Carlyle*

~ 58 ~

Lamentations 3:21 & 3:24 – *"This I recall to mind, therefore I have hope . . . The Lord is good to them that hope in Him, to those who seek Him."*

The more we have lost, the more we will appreciate Lamentations. It is not a book of the Bible that we automatically associate with hope. For some it is considered a dark and foreboding book about pain, injustice, and human loss. Even a casual reading of the five chapters clearly tells us why it is called Lamentations. The author Jeremiah sat weeping and lamenting over Jerusalem.

Still Jeremiah uses the word hope in the midst of all this doom and gloom. This third chapter represents a change in the prophet's emotions. So if we are in the midst of a period in our life where we can relate to Jeremiah's lamentations, it is time to relate to his hopefulness—it begins with remembrance. The prophet wanted to get out of his depression by thinking about the past. Sometimes that will help if we can recall good experiences, but often, as with Jeremiah, we dredge up the negatives and we feel worse. Let's review his outline for hope; notice first:

A New Recall – Jeremiah calls to remembrance God's faithfulness, and he begins to pull out of the quicksand of despair. It is always a matter of where we want to focus—if we focus on faith we move toward more hopelessness. Casey Stengel, legendary baseball manager, tells the story of a rookie pitcher. Having pitched the bases loaded, he was visited on the mound by Casey. "Focus on strikes. If you walk this guy, its back to the minors," shouted the manager to his youthful pitcher. After walking in the winning run, the rookie was interviewed by the press and he made this confession. "I was so scared by Mr. Stengel; I could only focus on his words: back to the MINORS." This illustrates how easy it is to focus on the negative. Our goal today is to focus on faith and to move toward hope.

The Lord's mercies are not consumed. His compassions fail not; they are new every morning. Great is your faithfulness.

I am sure the songwriter turned to Lamentations when he wrote "Great Is Thy Faithfulness." Thomas O. Chisholm had many disappointments in his life. Because of health issues he had to resign his pastorate as a Methodist preacher after just one year of service. Thomas enjoyed writing poetry and submitted them to various Christian publishers. Writing poetry produced only a meager income, and he made his living selling life insurance. At the age of seventy-five he wrote words that should inspire us today: "My income had never been large . . . because of poor health . . . but I must not fail to record the unfailing faithfulness of God . . . and His many displays of providing care." Thomas O. Chisholm did this in his greatest poem set to music in 1923. Review these words:

"GREAT is thy faithfulness. GREAT is thy faithfulness. Morning by morning new mercies I see. All I have needed thy hand hath provided. GREAT is thy faithfulness, Lord, unto me." Now that's hope!

> "The capacity for hope is the most significant fact of life; it gives us a sense of destination and the energy to get started." *–Norman Cousins*

~ 59 ~

Ezekiel 13:6 – *"And they made other to hope the Lord has not sent them."*

A false prophet. Not the most endearing term for anyone who suggests they speak for the Lord. Ezekiel lived in a time of many false prophets. He referred to them as foolish and like foxes in the desert. The imagery is that of a roving fox going through a city of ruin and desolation. The prophets are foolish because they are confusing their own message with that of the eternal God. Thus they are giving their followers "false hope." Foxes lived by being scavengers sifting through the remains of a ruined people. As did those prophets who have been referred to as "racketeers, not reformers."

Every generation of humankind has had to live with "false prophets." They, too, often have lived for their own profit and the loss of others. The hope they try to disseminate often leads to hopelessness and not an expectation of success. We all read in the media about Ponzi schemes. We are appalled that people could devise such evil plans to take advantage of their fellow human beings. But we should be even more appalled by those false prophets who manipulate fellow believers in the name of the Lord.

Today's devotion should encourage us not to be seduced by those who bring false hope. Sometimes it can be a TV personality, an author, a local preacher, or a gifted evangelist—all quite convincing, but quite false. The spiritual antennae should go up, and red flags should appear if they have a "new revelation" directly from God. The Scriptures tell us to "test the spirits" (1 John 4:1). We only need to review the many who have arrogantly and incorrectly given us a date for the end of the world. Our hope should come from those prophets sent from the Lord who continue to confirm "the faith once and forever delivered to the saints" (Jude 3).

There are a few telling signs we can look for in the false prophet (or cult):

• Does the prophet proclaim that they only have the revealed truth and that others before them are false?
• Does the prophet assume that they have new teachings (even beyond the Bible) that are to be accepted as gospel?
• Does the prophet require total allegiance to them, including time, talent, and finances? Usually they are au-

thoritative and control freaks. Obviously, they are peddlers of false hope.

The antidote, the cure, the alternative is Ezekiel's words "hear the Word of the Lord." The more we read the Word, study the Word, hear the Word, the more we have hope.

"The day the Lord created Hope was probably the same day He created spring." *—Bern Williams*

~ 60 ~

Ezekiel 19:5 (NKJV) – *"When she saw that she waited, that her hope was lost, She took another of her cubs and made him a young lion."*

Many of us enjoyed the film and message of the motion picture, The Lion King. It chronicles the life and experiences of the "king of the jungle." Disney's animated production was so popular it was returned to the screen in 3D. Generations of people have used the line, "the king of the jungle" as an image of bravery, courage, and leadership. Remember, Jesus is referred to as the Lion of the tribe of Judah (Revelation 5:5). In C.S. Lewis's classic *Tales of Narnia*, we see Jesus as the regal lion, Aslan. He calls upon the children to help him protect Narnia from evil and restore the throne to its rightful line. Today Ezekiel is writing about the nation of Israel and especially "a lamentation for the princes of Israel." The princes referred to are actually the kings of Judah, raised by the "mother lion" Israel.

If you enjoy history, you can dig into this quick review of Judah and Israel with the analogy of a lioness raising her cubs. The mother lion nourishes her young and teaches them to hunt prey. But it does not go well for her offspring. One cub (king) is brought in chains to Egypt; another is trapped in a pit. Disaster after disaster leads to invasion of Babylon and exile. Thus the verse of the day: "Her hope was lost." Can you relate?

Each of us has had times when hope seemed lost. Obviously not on the scale of Israel and Judah, but for our personal experiences it seemed immense. Ezekiel himself ended up in exile. He describes this as a spiritual wilderness, a dry and thirsty land. The good news is that although the Jews had once again deserted God, God had not deserted them. Like the mother lion looking after her cub, God was still going to raise Judah and nourish this rebellious land. Hope is needed in the time of our spiritual wilderness. We can relate to being in a dry and thirsty land because of spiritual rebellion. But now it is time for hope— for times of refreshment, for showers of blessings. How often in my ministry I have been blessed to cry out to God for showers of blessing, not just raindrops but showers, downpours, flood-gate storms. Today seek God's nourishment in prayer, Bible study, and fellowship with believers, and sharing our faith.

- Have you ever been just sitting there and all of a sudden you feel like doing something nice for someone you care for? THAT'S GOD. He talks to you through the Holy Spirit.
- Have you ever been down and out and nobody seems to be around for you to talk to? THAT'S GOD. He wants you to talk to Him.
- Have you ever been in a situation and you had no clue how it was going to get better, but now you look back on

it and see how it did? THAT'S GOD. He passes us through tribulation to see a brighter day.

In all that we do, we should totally give HIM thanks, and our blessings will continue to multiply.

Don't tell GOD how big your storm is; tell the storm how big your GOD is!

"Hope is the medicine I use more than any other; hope can cure nearly everything." –*Dr. McNair Wilson*

~ 61 ~

Ezekiel 37:11 (NKJV) – *"Then He said to me, 'Son of man, these bones are the whole house of Israel. They indeed say, "Our bones are dry, our hope is lost, and we ourselves are cut off!"'"*

Now the Jews are in captivity in Babylon. A century earlier, around 721 BC, the kingdom of Israel had come to its end. The Assyrians had conquered the people of God. Within one hundred short years, the Babylonians would then overthrow the Assyrians. Ezekiel himself has been taken captive along with the king. While there in Babylon, he has a number of remarkable vision—visions directly from the Lord, rebuking Israel for her rebellion against God. One of those visions was the "dry bones," probably one of the most well-known visions of the Bible.

Notice the vision of dry bones concerns the whole house of

Israel. Sometimes this has been used to describe the church, but for Ezekiel, it is the nation of God's people. A great army is to be brought back to life in the valley of dry bones. A scattered nation will eventually be brought back from the other nations and live again as a nation under God. But today's verse can speak only of bones being dried up, hope gone, and cut off. Only when the spirit of God enters the dry bones will things change.

Can you imagine what the prophet Ezekiel felt as these prophesies flowed through him? Can you imagine what the people thought as they had the prophesies communicated to them? Imagine for a moment your nation, your people, living in exile in a foreign land. Of course you pray for help. Was there going to be a future for the people of God? Ezekiel's message was to bring hope for a time when the scattered bones will be brought together as a living body. There are some who believe this gathering took place in 1947 when Jews returned to their homeland. Others believe it is the future Messianic kingdom. The northern and southern kingdom will be restored, and God will rule among them. For today's study, let's think of the church as either dry bones or living bones. Consider this reading…

LIVE CHURCHES have space problems—parking, classrooms, etc.
Dead churches have no worries about space.

LIVE CHURCHES are changing things;
Dead churches don't have to; they just stay the same.

LIVE CHURCHES have a shortage of staff;
Dead churches usually have a surplus.

LIVE CHURCHES have a problem developing new leaders; Dead churches don't; they just use the same ones over and over.

LIVE CHURCHES spend much on missions;
Dead churches keep it all home.

LIVE CHURCHES are filled with givers;
Dead churches are filled with tippers.

LIVE CHURCHES operate primarily on faith;
Dead churches operate totally on sight.

LIVE CHURCHES strain to learn and serve;
Dead churches seek rest and comfort.

LIVE CHURCHES evangelize;
Dead churches fossilize!

Pray today that God will put flesh on the bones of the church and each Christian believer.

"Dem-bones, Dem-bones, Dem-dry bones gonna walk around. Now hear the word of the Lord." *–Old Spiritual*

~ 62 ~

Hosea 2:15 (NKJV) – *"I will give her vineyards from there, and the Valley of Achor as a door of hope."*

Hosea would be a great proper name for a person; from the

Hebrew, it means salvation. The author is a prophet whose major message is the restoration of Israel. He has a message of salvation for his people during the eighth century BC. The message is given through his marriage to a prostitute, Gomer. Gomer is unfaithful to her husband, Hosea, as Israel is to God. In spite of her infidelities, Hosea continues to love her.

Today's verse takes us to a message of hope in an otherwise troubling prophecy. We are taken to a valley in a wilderness. (Not the picture of a place to find hope.) Most of the time we associate hope with a beautiful green pasture or majestic mountain tops, not with valleys in a wilderness. But that is the blessings of a God of hope. He will give us a door of hope even in the Valley of Achor. This valley had bad memories for Israel, dating back to its entry into Palestine. Bad memories can often take away our hope.

Reinhold Niebuhr wrote these words, "Grant us the serenity to accept the things we cannot change, the courage to change the things we can change, and the wisdom to know the difference." Now no doubt if you are anything like me, there are a lot of things in life that frustrate and discourage you day by day because you can't change them—like Hosea and his wife, Gomer. And then you realize there are things that everyone faces, conditions that are just impossible to change. All people have valleys. The difference is that some people cope with them more successfully than others; they cope with hope.

The late Thomas Kincaid, known as the artist of light, wrote: "One rainy afternoon I was driving along one of the main streets of town, taking those extra precautions necessary when the roads are wet and slick. Suddenly, my daughter, Aspen, spoke up from her relaxed position in her seat. 'Dad, I'm thinking of something.' This announcement usually meant she had been pondering some fact for a while and was now ready to expound all that her six-year-old mind had discovered. I was eager to hear. 'What are you thinking?' I asked. 'The rain,' she began, 'is like sin, and the windshield wipers are like God wiping our sins away.' After the chill bumps raced up my arms, I was able to respond. 'That's really good, Aspen.' Then my curiosity broke in. How far would this little girl take this revelation? So I asked, 'Do you notice how the rain keeps on coming? What does that tell you?' Aspen didn't hesitate one moment with her answer: 'We keep sinning, and God just keeps on forgiving us.'"

Of course, this can be taken to the extreme and justify continual sinning, but that is not the point. Our message today is to confront our Valleys of Achor with the positive knowledge that we succeed and progress spiritually because of "the door of hope."

"I find hope in the darkest of days and focus on the brightest." *–Dalai Lama*

~ 63 ~

Joel 3:16 (KJV) – *"The Lord will be the hope of his people."*

Prophets had a "profitable" message for the people of God. But the message could also be quite frightening. They could inspire, but they could also condemn and warn of judgment. If you enjoy reading about a prophet who personally knew of God's work and power, read all three chapters of this Old Testament book of Joel.

Our verse of Scripture on hope comes after Joel's speaking of an invasion from locusts—total destruction of all crops. This still happens today in many third-world countries (even in the USA). You can imagine, however, how devastating such an invasion was during ancient times. Because of the loss of their main economic source, priests are in mourning as humanity seems to wither away. People are called upon to repent in sackcloth; a holy fast is called. But in all of this, the message of hope is sounded by Joel—a popular verse often used as a call to revival—"I will repay you the years the locusts have eaten" (Joel 2:25).

Today we are concerned about sexual promiscuity; imagine what it was like for our Lord to see his people trading boys for prostitutes, selling girls for wives. Talk about evil. Joel saw it to the maximum. But the important message is that our Lord does judge sin. He will not wink at it. Joel reverses the words of Isaiah and writes, "Beat your plow shears into swords and the pruning hooks into spears." Yet the Lord's people will be blessed in spite of these events, if their hope will remain in God.

Every age needs it prophets. Sometimes they will be condemned; sometimes people will realize they are right and will listen. Today we may be going through a "time of the locusts." A few years ago our beautiful oak trees were devastated by gypsy moths. Like locusts with insatiable appetites, the gypsies stripped trees bare of leaves, leaving them vulnerable to death. Eventually we were able to fight them with aerial pesticides that saved the trees, but some were lost. All around us today are forces that would destroy the church, impede the gospel, and cause spiritual death. In some ways it is like a plight of locusts or an invasion of gypsy moths. It is time for us to be spiritual prophets that bring hope to a weary land.

"Determine now that each day you will go beyond a search for hope, to a deeper search for God. Then you will have hope." *–Roger C. Palms*

~ 64 ~

Zechariah 9:12 (NKJV) – *"Return to the stronghold, you prisoners of hope."*

It was a remarkable sight on television—the grainy black-and-white images of men and women being released from imprisonment in a foreign country. They had endured torture, isolation, interrogation, separation from family, and even threats of death, but now they were free. Military escorts awaited them to take each of the prisoners to an airport and a long flight home. If a TV camera were available in 520 BC, we could see images of the prophet Zechariah and the people as word came from Cyrus the King of Babylon that the Jews could go free and return to Jerusalem.

Can you envision the celebrations and absolute joy that the Jews felt going home, going back to their people, back to the temple, back to Jerusalem? The stronghold! But Zechariah realized the trip back would not be easy. He had been born in captivity and grew up in exile. Surrounded by people who felt hopeless, he probably was tempted to quit. But Zechariah was an encourager and motivator. It was his ambition to return so they could re-build the temple. The people would need daily encouragement and motivation to complete their plans. Thus he referred to them as "prisoners of hope." Released from the prisons of Babylon, they would become "prisoners of hope."

As you read this today, you may need to be released from the prison of Babylon. Doubt, sin, debilitating habits, anxiety, and fear—all can rob us of hope. We need to focus on returning to the stronghold of our faith. Maybe we need to get back to church, Bible study, fellowship with the believers, and daily devotion. The prophet Zechariah has a word of hope—expectation of success—for our generation. Let's take his encouragement and motivation seriously today. Keep in mind, the Jews at first approached their work with great enthusiasm (haven't we all), but soon they encountered many obstacles. Zechariah as prophet and priest had to give them a vision even beyond the restored temple. Read the entire 9th chapter and get blessed.

"Many believe—and I believe—that I have been designated for this work by God. In spite of my old age, I do not want to give it up. I work out of love for God, and I put all my hope in Him." —*Michelangelo*

~ 65 ~

Luke 6:34–35 – *"And if you lend to those from whom you hope to receive back, what credit is that to you? . . . But love your enemies do good to them and lend to them without hoping to get anything back."*

Luke is recording many of the passages recorded in Matthew as the Sermon on the Mount. In this record Jesus is on a plateau on a mountain (a level place), and it is a shorter version of the Sermon on the Mount. However, the theme is the same: our walk as a follower of Jesus. There are some challenging teachings from our Savior telling us how to walk the walk.

After speaking of the Sabbath, performing miracles, and reciting the beatitudes (or as some have called them "the blessed attitudes"), Jesus focuses on loving our enemies and even speaks of issues like lending money. That's right, "lending money." I think all of us have been in a position of lending money to someone. Jesus challenges his followers with an important spiritual principle: don't just lend money with the hope you'll get it back. In a sense, lend it to help, lend it to bless; that should be our motivation.

I learned this the hard way. A coworker came to me and needed a cosigner to get a car. The bank made the loan; my signature guaranteed its repayment. He was a fellow believer, had a good work ethic, and convinced me there was no risk. His wife and children were also involved in ministry, and without hesitation I signed the "note." Now fast forward—one year after the loan— he left his wife, quit his job, left the area, took the car, and I was left to honor the note. A banker friend who knew of the situation said, "Dave, you save the souls; let us loan the money."

Now on the surface that is good advice, but in the context of today's Scripture on hope, it is poor Christianity. Should I go out and take risks with my hard-earned financial resources? Of course not! Should I be an enabler for those who are poor managers of their life or money? Of course not! But when I can help a brother or sister in Christ during a time of financial need, I will do it not hoping (expecting) to get it back but because I am in a position to be a blessing. The blessing comes from the giving, not the getting back. By the way, most people I've helped have returned the money, so I can then bless another. Why let the banks have all the fun?

"Once you choose hope, anything is possible."
–*Christopher Reeve*

~ **66** ~

Luke 23:8 – *"Herod hoped to see Jesus perform miracles."*

Herod—a name that conjures up all kinds of images. This is the infamous Herod Antipas. You remember—the one who beheaded John the Baptist. (Nice guy.) Now he has come to Jerusalem to keep the Passover, as governor of Galilee. Pilate has sent Jesus to Herod, hoping that the governor would either punish Jesus or release him. We call it passing the buck, or kicking the stone down the road for someone else to make a decision. Jesus was from Galilee, so Pilate decided Herod should have this responsibility.

As Luke writes his gospel, he gives us an interesting insight into Herod and Jesus. Herod wants to see Jesus. Obviously Herod had heard about this rabbi from Galilee, and as Luke writes, "He was desirous to see him." Why? To see him perform some miracles. Herod asks Jesus questions, in fact, question after question. It would be interesting to know what his inquiries were—we can only conjecture—but whatever they were, Jesus did not give an answer. Herod must have been extremely agitated because he (along with his soldiers) begin to mock and ridicule Jesus. They even dressed him in an elegant robe and send him back to Pilate. Luke adds an interesting footnote to the story by saying that Pilate and Herod became friends that day, having formerly been enemies. (Politics and evil make strange bedfellows.)

King Herod's song in Jesus Christ Superstar (Broadway show from 1971) captures this inquisitive leader in the ironic lyrics. He tells Jesus that he is happy to meet him, but Jesus needs to prove Himself to the ruler. He taunts Christ as the King of the Jews and then dismisses him. Herod's hope was based upon a total misunderstanding of Jesus and His gospel.

This negative is a message for all of us; our hope cannot be based upon Jesus performing some magic or spiritual tricks just for our amusement or amazement. Our hope is built upon the Savior, His life, His gospel, His death for our sins, and His resurrection. Herod never experienced the real Jesus in his life; we can! "Come into my life, King of the Jews. Come into my life, you the Christ."

> "What oxygen is to the lungs, such is hope to the meaning of life." *–Emil Brunner*

~ 67 ~

Luke 24:21 (NIV) – *"We had hoped that he was the one who was going to redeem Israel."*

The painting of the Emmaus Road is a favorite. Jesus is walking with two followers and they don't recognize him. As I look at the painting, I imagine myself in the scene. Emmaus, a small village, is about seven miles from Jerusalem. (No short hike for anyone.) Some amazing events have taken place in Jerusalem, and the followers have been involved in a conversation about those events when Jesus joins them. Like the two of them, I'm sure I would not have realized who was with us. Jesus had been crucified, and as far as they were concerned, he was no longer alive, and their hope of a redeemer for Israel was dashed.

Sadly, two thousand years later, there are still many who do not believe Jesus is the Redeemer. Like the two on the Emmaus Road, they do not recognize the Savior. Some do not believe in a Messiah; others are still waiting and watching. One follower that day was named Cleopas. He is described as being downcast. Even after the women told him the tomb was empty, Cleopas seemed to have no hope. When we are hopeless, we do become downcast. We are often miserable to all around us.

But thank God the story doesn't end there. Jesus eventually shares a meal. It is at that time they realize who He is, and they say, "Our hearts burned within us as He talked with us on the road and opened the Scripture. At meal time the light of hope went on. It was Jesus who had walked with them." They then went back to Jerusalem to tell the others that Jesus was alive and had risen.

Did you ever read a mythological story of Jesus retiring to heaven? Those in heaven who believed he was crucified and had been defeated confront Him with that accusation. Jesus responds, "I have not been defeated. I have left my followers to carry on." The critics then say, "Ah, but Jesus, suppose those followers fail?" With intensity in his voice, Jesus responds, "If my followers fail, I have no other plans." No other plans. Today we are His plans. There are many on the modern-day Emmaus Road, and we need to help them see Jesus. Hope can help our hearts to burn within us.

Prayer – "Eternal God, send your Spirit to strengthen those who have no strength, to bring peace to those who have no peace, and give hope to all in despair. Amen."
—*Carol Griffin*

~ 68 ~

Acts 2:26 (NIV) – *"Therefore my heart is glad and my tongue rejoices; my body also will rest in hope."*

The book of Acts is a history book. It is an exciting history book written by the physician Luke. If you like history, you will find Acts the book of action, telling what happened to the church after the resurrection of Jesus. Some scholars consider it a sequel to the Gospels, from Pentecost to Paul preaching in Rome. But in between those two events we find the stories of Paul, the difficulties faced by the young church, and today's record of a sermon preached by Peter at Pentecost.

Get the picture—the Holy Spirit has come upon the disciples in Jerusalem. It is an awesome event with a sound like a rushing wind, tongues of fire appearing, and people speaking in other tongues. Is it any wonder Luke records that the gathering crowd was bewildered and amazed? (I probably would have "freaked out.") Add to that, the people could understand each other even though they spoke in different languages. Some wanted to know what all this meant, and others just said, "You're drunk." It was up to Peter to address the crowd and interpret what was happening. The sermon Peter preached contains today's words of hope, "My heart is glad, therefore my body will also live [rest] in hope."

But keep in mind that he is quoting David, and David is referring to the Messiah. Again picture the scene. Peter is the first disciple to recognize Jesus as the Messiah and tries to help the people understand what has just happened. Remember, some of them thought everyone was drunk. Peter has to give meaning to the event. So he quotes the prophet Joel and God's promise that those who follow Him would receive the Spirit. Peter takes the narrative right to Jesus and His fulfilling the promise when he sends the Holy Spirit on his disciples. You can image how the listener was intrigued when he quotes Psalm 16:8–11, stating the Messiah will not decay, not be left in Sheol; he will be at the right hand of God.

So we arrive at today's hope. As the Messiah will not stay in the grave, nor will His body decay, so this is also our hope. We will put on a new body! Think of that for a moment. I used to joke that I wanted to be as tall as Wilt Chamberlain, as handsome as Robert Redford, and well-built like Arnold Schwarzenegger. Now that would be a new body! But obviously that is not what Peter is referring to. We put on a new spiritual body. On a more serious level, I have also thought of our oldest daughter Lee Ann. She was born with multiple birth defects and never walked. My wife and I have often shared the glorious hope that at her death she put on a new body. No wheelchair, no leg braces, no shunts—a new spiritual body that she inhabits for eternity; her heart is glad.

Today we ask, is that your hope? Are you now filled with God as the Holy Spirit? We may believe in God as the father, creator, and sustainer of the universe, we may believe in Jesus as our personal Savior, but now we want to also believe that the Holy Spirit fills us with the power and energy of God. The world may think we are drunk, but it is the path to a glad heart and a new body that lives forever.

"Consult not your fear but your hopes and dreams. Concern yourself not with what you tried and failed in, but what is still possible to do." *–Pope John XXIII*

~ **69** ~

Acts 16:19 (KJV) – *"The hope of their gains was gone."*

She was a fortune teller—not one with a crystal ball or tarot cards, but one who had what the Bible story calls a "spirit of divination." Notice Paul and Silas are on their way to pray when they meet her. Paul knew this was not a gift from God, but rather an evil spirit had possessed the young woman. Paul demanded the demon leave her, and it did "in the name of Jesus."

But now complications took place. The young woman had been used by her master for financial income. They profited from her possession. Whatever the sources of the power she had for future telling, it was now cut off. She had been freed; they had been busted. Like a modern sexual pimp that has one of his woman changed and brought to Christ, the masters were furious. The hope of their gains was gone.

Evil people also have their hopes. Predicated on the wrong values, their expectation of success often manipulates others and builds on their weaknesses. This story has an important message for all of us. Things are to be used, not people. Using people for our own personal gain will have tragic results. Hope is of a more positive persuasion.

As you read the sixteenth chapter of Acts, you will note the story doesn't end here. Paul and Silas were taken by the girls' masters to the local magistrate. They end up being charged for going against Roman traditions, are severely beaten, thrown into jail, and their feet are put in shackles. So much for freeing a young woman from demon possession. It went counterculture against the norm of the day.

But wait, in case you are wondering where the hope is, make sure you read verses 25–34. There was a keeper of the jail who was responsible for keeping Paul and Silas in jail. He heard them singing hymns, an earthquake took place, the prison doors are opened, and that night the jailer and his entire family are brought to Christ. And when daylight came, he made the decision to let Paul and Silas out of jail! The jailer discovered that the two of them were Roman citizens and had all the rights and privileges that went with them.

Are you exhausted from this memorable history lesson? It helps us remember there are those who have hope for evil, but there are those who have hope for the best! The young woman was now a woman of hope, the jailer and his family were people of hope, and now those of us living generations later can rejoice that the hope of our gains is not lost.

> "Little progress can be made by merely attempting to re-press what is evil. Our great hope lies in developing what is good." –*Calvin Coolidge*

~ 70 ~

Acts 23:6 (KJV) – *"The hope and resurrection of the dead."*

Fast forward as church history continues to unfold. Luke is now focused on Paul and his amazing ministry as a missionary. Reading this condensation of events is like a thrilling novel, but we know it is all true. Paul is once again threatened with death, escapes an unruly mob, appeals to his Roman citizenship, and ends up on trial before the Sanhedrin! It is at this time that Paul rebukes the high priest and then repents of being disrespectful to the ruler.

Remember when we wrote about the Sadducees? Well, as Paul goes on trial he notes that his judges are divided between Sadducees and Pharisees. It is a division that Paul takes advantage of. The Pharisees believe in the resurrection, and Paul witnesses to the fact that he is a Pharisee: "I am a Pharisee, the son of a Pharisee, and I am being tried because I have the hope of the resurrection from the dead." Debate raged between the warring Jewish factions. Paul's strategy worked, Paul was taken to a castle for protection, and that night "the Lord stood by him."

People are still deeply divided over the resurrection of the dead. Contemporary agnostics, atheists, or those of other religious persuasions question the Christian belief in eternal life. A well-known atheist of the twenty-first century, Christopher Hitchens, after learning of his terminal illness, still wanted everyone to know it had not changed his belief system. If he had a deathbed conversion, it would be because he had become mentally incompetent. Conversely his brother, Peter Hitchens, also a brilliant intellect, had become a Christian, and his greatest hope was for his brother to know the reality of heaven. Tragically, Christopher died without any public acknowledgment of his conversion.

Eternal life is our ultimate hope. It is a goal of every believer, our crowning expectation of success. D.L. Moody, forerunner to Billy Sunday and Billy Graham, had an incredible ministry. Someone once remarked, "D.L. Moody depopulated hell by two million people." In a more positive sense, two million people reached heaven because of his preaching the gospel. Moody said before his death, "When you read that D.L. Moody is dead, don't believe it. I'll be more alive than I am at this moment." Hope can do that to you.

"Nothing that is worth doing can be achieved in a lifetime; therefore we must be saved by hope." –*Reinhold Niebuhr*

~ 71 ~

Acts 24:15 (KJV) – *"And have hope toward God."*

Paul has had a very busy time defending himself and the faith. It has not been an easy time or a pleasant experience. Consider that in just a few days he went from a time in the temple praying to an appearance before the Sanhedrin, prison, saw an appearance of the Lord, had forty Jews plot to kill him, had soldiers take him to Antipas, and now he is brought to Caesarea to appear before Felix. If that isn't enough, add to that a leading orator, Tertulus, who addresses the crowd. Tertulus argues that Paul is really in charge of sedition among the Jews (he is a terrorist) and a renegade of the group called the Nazarenes. Think you have had a bad week?

Remarkably, this turns into an opportunity for Paul to witness to Felix the governor. It is no small miracle that he is brought there safely by two hundred foot soldiers, seventy cavalry, and two centurions. Quite a guard for one little Jewish prisoner, who had claimed Roman citizenship. Oh, and by the way, he also had a letter of introduction, so Felix knew the accusations being brought. But Felix made a glaring mistake—he offered Paul a time to speak, and speak he did. This became Paul's testimony time.

Acts 24:15 is part of Paul's defense; he has hope toward God. His hope comes from his roots in Judaism. He has not been preaching anything heretical or seditious. He is worshipping the God of his father, believing the law and the prophets. "Those people who brought charges against me should be here if they found me to be evil," he says to Felix. And then he reveals the real reason for all the fuss. "I'm here because we differ in the teaching about the resurrection of the dead." Is it any wonder Felix stops the proceedings? Paul is given some liberty until the experiences with Governor Felix continue —to the point where even the governor's wife, Drusilla, (a Jewess) hears Paul's testimony.

How does this factor into our hope for today? Religious, governmental, or cultural leaders should not dissuade us from the faith once and forever given to the saints. There is always pressure from various secular and religious agencies to have us water down our faith. Issues like life and death, marriage, freedom to evangelize, access to media, and hiring practices can come in conflict with "those in power" and the faith community. Today we have our roots—deep down in the soil of the gospel, two thousand years of hope. Each generation having to stand firm like Paul and have hope toward God!

"Hope lies in dreams, in imagination, and in the courage of those to make dreams into reality." *–Jonas Salk*

~ 72 ~

Acts 24:26 – *"Hoping for a bribe from Paul."*

This is probably one of the most unusual uses of the word hope we will find in the Bible. "Hoping for a BRIBE" is used in relationship to Felix, a provincial governor. This political leader is no stranger to followers of Christ, who were then known as followers of the Way. But who would have guessed that Felix wanted a payoff to release Paul? Let's look at his other misadventures, and we see a pattern.

Felix had been governor of Judea and Samaria for six years. He was married to Drusilla, who was Jewish. She was the great-granddaughter of Herod the Great. You remember the infamous Herod the Great? This was the Herod who tried to kill the baby Jesus. Wait, there is more to the family tree. She was the great niece of another Herod who killed John the Baptist. Her father was the man who had the Apostle James put to death. So now let's look at her husband Felix!

When Felix met Drusilla, she was already married. Her husband was the king of Emesa in Syria. But this would not stop the egocentric politician. Felix had already been married twice. Hold on for this tabloid exposure. His first wife was the granddaughter of Mark Antony and Cleopatra—nice genes—and his second wife had been a princess. Both former wives were now history and divorced. It is to this couple, Felix and Drusilla, that

Paul speaks about righteous living, being self-centered, and the coming judgment. Paul must have touched some major nerve because Felix is afraid and tells Paul to "go away for now; come back at a better time."

A term that used to be common in evangelical churches is "under conviction." It described a person who admitted their sin and was ready to make a profession of faith in Christ as their Savior. Some students of the Bible believe Felix was close but missed the opportunity. Remember, Paul was talking to a man noted for his ruthlessness. Tacitus, an ancient historian, wrote about Felix, "He practiced every kind of cruelty and lust." This is the person who hoped to get a bribe so he would free Paul.

Two years would pass with Felix in his position as governor. He would have other conversations with Paul, but after he was succeeded by Porcius Festus, he did the Jews a favor and kept Paul in prison. His hope for a bribe never came to be. Paul was later sent to Rome because he proved he was a Roman citizen. Keep in mind Felix wanted to talk about a payoff; Paul wanted to talk about the Lord.

This story illustrates the age-old struggles of the human spirit. Do we place our hope in man's natural instincts to bribe and manipulate, or do we trust the God who grants us His amazing grace and forgiveness? Felix continued to do evil. He was removed from office because of the way he crushed a riot in Caesarea. He was vicious. So much for placing our hope in the wrong place. Today, this moment, seek the God of hope who gives us expectation of success, not failure. Felix is a prime example of failure; he should have listened to Paul.

"No one is hopeless whose hope is in God and His Word." *–Phillip Yancy*

~ 73 ~

Acts 26:6–7 (KJV) – *"And now I stand and am judged for the hope of the promise made of God, unto our fathers"*

It was one thing to be on trial before Felix, the governor, but now Paul stands before King Agrippa. He is the representative of Rome, often called a Herodian King. (Interesting that his name literally means "one causing pain.") He hears about Paul through Festus, a procurator that wanted to keep everyone happy. It was the Jews' hope to send Paul back to Jerusalem and on the way have him murdered. Festus vetoed the trip idea and ordered that Paul stay right there and appear before the king.

Once again the door is opened for "testimony time." Festus explains the case against Paul brought by the Jews. He doesn't think it has much validity but the King should hear from Paul directly. Imagine what went through Paul's mind when Agrippa said, "Thou art permitted to speak for thyself." No lawyer needed, no stand in. Paul, in your own words, talk to me! Thus Paul begins his classic defense before the king. He starts with, "I think myself happy to appear before you," and then his words, which could be interpreted as, "I know you are an expert on Judaism."

Now if Agrippa thought this was going to be another dull defense from a guilty party, he was in for a rude awakening. Paul again talks about the resurrection of the dead, his life as a persecutor of the church, even overseeing people being put to death, and then he segues into his own conversation. It must have been high courtroom drama, bordering on the theater. His audience of judges and jury were listening to Paul's life story from the time he was raised as a strict Jewish Pharisee (a fundamentalist of the fundamentalists). He speaks of his conversion on the Damascus road, hearing the voice of Jesus, and his calling to open people's eyes to the truth of the Gospel. Is it any wonder Agrippa leaps up and shouts, "Paul, you are crazy. All this learning has made you mad." But it also led to King Agrippa's confessing, "Paul, you almost persuaded me to be a Christian."

We want to stand today and also be judged for the hope of the promise made of God unto our fathers! Whatever your Christian theology, your church history, your interpretation of Scripture, we have a hope of the promise to pass on. One night in a camp meeting message, I spoke of John Wesley and his ministry of preaching and showing social concerns for the poor and needy. One young man on the way out of the service said he didn't come for a history lesson; another shared how he was blessed to remember the Wesleyan traditions and how to revive them today. Check the promises made to you today. They will bring new hope for this generation.

> "Expect to have hope rekindled. Expect your prayers to be answered in wondrous ways. Dry seasons do not last!" *–Sarah Ban Breathnach*

~ 74 ~

Acts 27:20 (NIV) – *"We finally gave up all hope of being saved."*

Paul is on his way to Rome. He boards a ship that will take him from ports along the coast of Asia, to Sidon, Pamphylia, and Myra. Almost from the beginning, the trip confronts bad weather. They lose time because of rough seas and treacherous winds. Paul warns the seamen that they should seek a good harbor and remain there for the winter, but his captors and the pilot of the ship do not listen. Hold on for an amazing adventure that caused many to give up hope.

Here in New Jersey we have a beautiful shoreline bordering the Atlantic Ocean. Boardwalks, amusement parks, beautiful homes, and businesses dot the landscape from north to south Jersey. Summertime people flock to "the beach" or the "shore" by the thousands to enjoy fun and sun. But a "northeaster" hit the central Jersey beaches in 2012, and the results were catastrophic. Millions of dollars in property damage, loss of life, and chaos visited the playgrounds of the garden state. It was a similar northeaster that dramatically changed Paul's trip to Rome and the lives of those who traveled with him.

Imagine yourself in the midst of a hurricane. The vessel you are on is so badly damaged that ropes are tied around the hull to try and hold it together. The anchor is thrown over to try and slow down the ship as it passes near dangerous sandbars. Cargo is thrown overboard, the battering from the storm is so bad. This goes on for three more days with neither the sun nor moon being visible for even more time. It is at this point that those on board the ship give up hope of being saved.

Have you ever reached that point in life? You may not have been on a ship at sea, but events in life have brought you to a place of no hope. It may have been in a hospital room, a boss's office, a church meeting, a divorce court, reading an obituary notice, receiving financial news—the list is endless. Whatever the event is, it is best for us to rewrite these words: we finally did not give up hope of being saved. Because now we continue in this chapter in Acts and read Paul's encouraging words.

"Men, I urge you to keep up your courage, because not one of you will be lost; only the ship will be destroyed. Last night an angel of God whose I am and who I serve, stood before me and said, 'Do not be afraid, so keep up your courage, _____ (put your name here), for I have faith in God that it will happen just as He told me.'"

Now I am sure those men were startled to hear this message of hope, just as we are. But we know the end of the story. They all eventually reached land safely. Hope changes people. It changes you and I. To paraphrase Winston Churchill, "Never, never, never give up hope."

> "The storm may roar without me, my heart may low be laid, but God is all around me, and I cannot be dismayed." –*Anna Waring*

~ 75 ~

Acts 28:20 (NIV) – *"It is because of the Hope of Israel that I am bound with this chain."*

Paul has had some amazing audiences. After returning to Rome, he calls together the leaders of the Jews. He has spoken to Agrippa, to Felix, to his guards, to fellow prisoners, and to anyone else who would listen. Now, still under guard, he takes this opportunity to again witness to his fellow Jews. He speaks of the kingdom of God and tries to convince them that Jesus is the Messiah, using the Law of Moses and the Prophets. Some believed, and of course some rejected his message. Keep in mind, all this time he is bound by a chain.

In Paul's mind, this chain is symbolic. If it were not for his great desire to share the gospel of hope to Israel, he wouldn't have that chain. After all, by the time he reaches Rome, he is a well-respected and trusted prisoner. That's right, he is still a prisoner of the Roman authorities. And during the last few months he has endured a shipwreck, listened as sailors planned a mutiny, survived a snake bite, and healed a Roman official's father. But he has a tough audience because Jews in Rome are already ostracized and don't want any more controversies.

In our world, chains are for animals or securing property. We chain our dog to the house, an elephant in the circus, a gate to keep in livestock, or a padlock on a fence around a property. It is difficult to relate to people being chained. But sometimes we can't see the chains that bind us. Samson, in the Old Testament, was a strong man who was chained and blinded before he realized the true source of his strength. Chains can have very negative connotations. People are chained to drugs, alcohol, crime—all types of perversion, often without the hope of the gospel. But for Paul, a chain was a badge of honor; it was because he was bringing hope to Israel. In one of Paul's letters, he writes of bearing in his body the marks of the Lord Jesus. The modern translation is, "I bear in my body the brands of the Lord Jesus." Wherever he would go to share the gospel, people would know he wanted wore chains and now was branded with a cross.

A modern day Paul was seen in the life of Chuck Colson. Chuck was incarcerated because of the Watergate debacle. He converted his "chains" into a ministry of hope for prisoners. From hatchet man for the Nixon administration, he became an evangelist and spokesman for those lost in the world of crime. Colson spread hope to prisoners and their families and has given us an example of one who brings an expectation of success. Although Chuck has now passed away, his ministry "Prison Fellowship" continues to function across our nation and around the world. Have you been bound by any chains for the glory of God? We, too, can bring hope to the world by bearing in our body the brand of the Lord Jesus.

"In our desert of grief, Jesus can provide an oasis of hope." *–Bill Crowder*

~ 76 ~

Romans 4:18 (KJV) – *"Who against hope believed in hope."*

Romans 4:18 seems, at first reading, to be a paradox. Paul is writing about Abraham and how the Jewish patriarch was justified before God. It is Abraham who against hope believed in hope. (Say what?) Actually, this becomes more clear if we translate it this way: "When Abraham was physically beyond any hope of having a child, he based his hope on God's promises instead." It was this hope that affirmed a belief his "offspring would be more numerous than the stars of heaven." For Abraham it was the all-powerful God that had promised it, and so against hope he believed in HOPE. Remember, both he and

his wife, Sarah, were beyond childbearing age when she conceived Isaac. Hope in today's culture is defined differently. For instance, in the media it is often a vague reference to wishful thinking. There is no faith foundation for using the word. But for a believer, hope is the hope of Abraham, not just a whimsical dream of the future. It is not hope in hope, as it is also not just faith in faith. Our hope is based on the reality of God.

Of course, our hope is often challenged by the events of life. When our first daughter was born with major birth defects, our hope was challenged. When she later died a horrific death, our hope was challenged. Events on the Ranch working with the youth, parents, law enforcement agencies, the courts, and the public have all brought moments of success and failure.

Personal illnesses, financial challenges, and family concerns have all taken their toll on remaining "hopeful." But there has been a verse of Scripture that always brings me back to focus: "In this world you will have tribulation; but be of good cheer. I have overcome the world" (John 16:33). Those words of Jesus help you and I who against hope believe in HOPE.

Study this outline I have shared called "The Confessions of the Founder of Ranch Hope." Five brief thoughts pinpoint how we have remained in this ministry for nearly fifty years. I hope they will also help you.

- *Stay focused* on Jesus – Avoid the peripheral issues of life that drain us.
- *Be faithful* – Keep trusting the one who calls us to follow Him. Like a good US Marine "Semper Fi," always be faithful.
- *Have fun* – Enjoy what you do for the Lord. Rejoice in the Lord always, and again I say rejoice.
- *Remember the finances* – It takes money to support the work of the Lord. Be a cheerful giver and do your givin' while you're livin' so you're knowin' where its goin'.
- *Finish what you start.* – Complete the running of the race for our Lord.

"Do not pray for tasks equal to your prayers, but for power equal to your tasks." *–Phillips Brooks*

~ 77 ~

Romans 5:2 (NKJV) – *"And rejoice in hope."*

146

The church of Rome had little in which to rejoice. Talk about persecution—they could write a textbook on the subject. History records the atrocities against the first-century believers; they lived each day under the threat of Nero and his sadistic subjects. Paul was well aware of this and was, himself, under constant threat, but writes, "Rejoice in hope." (Remember he also writes, "Rejoice in the Lord always, and again I say Rejoice." The emphasis is for every reader.)

Many believe this is the most important section of the letter. Paul takes us from our being "justified" by faith, the first step in our spiritual growth to peace, and then our hope in the glory of God. Wow, what a wonderful progression. No wonder we can rejoice in hope. Roman persecution, life's frailties, the human condition, nothing negates our rejoicing in hope!

John Bunyan, author of *Pilgrim's Progress,* has a character, Mr. Steadfast, who remarks, "The big courage is the cold blooded kind, the kind that never lets go when you're feeling empty inside, and your blood's thin, and there's no kind of fun or profit to be had, and the trouble's not over in an hour or two but lasts for months and years. One of the men here was speaking about that kind and he called it 'fortitude.' I reckon fortitude's the biggest thing a man can have—just to go on enduring when there's no guts or heart left in you, but the head man at the job was the apostle Paul."

The apostle Paul is a mentor of hope for each of us. As Mister Steadfast remarks, "Paul is the head man at the job." Every job needs a head man, a manager, a leader. His example should encourage all of us even through our most horrific circumstances. It is still difficult to imagine all that Paul endured as an apostle. An apostle is someone sent to represent another. In this case, he was sent to represent the Lord Jesus. We are also sent, and Paul as our mentor has left us a testimony of endurance.

Today we rejoice in hope, not because all is well, but because of the glory of God. Pray this prayer and focus on hope today:

> "God of compassion, send your Spirit to strengthen those who have no strength, to bring peace to them who have no peace, and to give hope to all in despair. Amen."
> *–Carol Griffin*

~ 78 ~

Romans: 5:3–4 (KJV) – *"We glory in tribulations also: knowing that tribulation worketh patience; and patience, experience; and experience, hope."*

Notice the process of moving from "rejoicing in our sorrows" (NIV) to patience, to experience, to hope. Quite a transition and a pattern of spiritual growth. Paul has been writing about our justification by faith. It will become a major foundation block of Christian teaching. A common method of teaching this is to say justification means "just as if I never sinned." When I place faith in Christ, I am a new creature and the past is the past. But now we build on that foundation and move toward hope.

It is never easy to glory in tribulations (rejoice in sorrow). Human nature dictates otherwise. In fact, it seems unnatural for Paul to write such a teaching. But there are believers who have reached that goal. A few years ago, a good friend became a pilot. Most of his adult life had been spent on the ocean navigating small yachts back and forth from New Jersey to Florida.

In fact, he even built his own yacht that he and his family enjoyed sailing. Later he developed a passion to fly, and thus he had the best of both worlds, sea and sky.

One afternoon he began a flight out west for a hunting trip. He and his son boarded the small, single-engine plane on an overcast day. They took off from an airfield close to home. His wife accompanied her husband and son to the plane, said her goodbyes, and watched as the plane took off. Minutes later, there was a horrific crash, and father and son were killed.

The next few days were a test of all of us who knew and loved this little boy and his father. You can imagine the tribulation that his wife endured. A strong Christian woman was crushed with a double loss but became an encouragement to her family and friends who knew both the husband and the son. Without saying the exact words, she was living out Paul's teaching under the most difficult and trying circumstances. From tribulation to patience to experience to hope.

Now fast forward three years. I recently received correspondence from the widow, who is also a dear friend, and she told of plans to go on a mission trip with others in her church, a mission trip to work with others and share the gospel of hope. That is what can happen to all who experience tribulations. Paul was not speaking as some classroom theologian. He was not a poet or prose writer developing some beautiful rhyme. For him this was a living, breathing reality. From an airplane crash wiping out her family to mission work—what a memorial to her husband and son, passing on the expectation of success for those who love Jesus.

"The hope of all who seek Him, the help of all who find." –*Alfred H. Ackley "He Lives"*

~ 79 ~

Romans 8:20 (NKJV) – *"For the creation was subjected to futility, not willingly, but because of Him who subjected it in hope."*

Let's start with "the creation was subjected to futility," which literally means "vanity or emptiness." Paul reminds the church that we live in a fallen creation. From the time of Adam and Eve's rebellion, we are living under a curse. Recently I received this e-mail with a rather humorous take on this condition:

Recall Notice:
The maker of all human beings (GOD) is recalling all units manufactured, regardless of make or year, due to a serious defect in the primary and central component of the heart.

This is due to a malfunction in the original prototype units code named Adam and Eve, resulting in the reproduction of the same defect in all subsequent units. This defect has been technically termed "Sub-sequential Internal Non-Morality," or more commonly known as S.I.N., as it is primarily expressed.

Some of the symptoms include:
1. Loss of direction
2. Foul vocal emissions

3. Amnesia of origin
4. Lack of peace and joy
5. Selfish or violent behavior
6. Depression or confusion in the mental component
7. Fearfulness
8. Idolatry
9. Rebellion

The manufacturer, who is neither liable nor at fault for this defect, is providing factory-authorized repair and service free of charge to correct this defect.

With that in mind, Paul introduces hope. Hope for a fallen world. Read on to verse 21: "Because the creation itself also will be delivered from the bondage of corruption into the glorious liberty of the children of God." Now continue with the e-mail. It is lighthearted, but it is the hope for the world's condition.

The repair technician, JESUS, has most generously offered to bear the entire burden of the staggering cost of these repairs. There is no additional fee required. The number to call for repair in all areas is: P-R-A-Y-E-R.

Once connected, please upload your burden of SIN through the REPENTANCE procedure. Next, download ATONEMENT from the repair technician, Jesus, into the heart component.

No matter how big or small the SIN defect is, Jesus will replace it with:
1. Love
2. Joy

3. Peace
4. Patience
5. Kindness
6. Goodness
7. Faithfulness
8. Gentleness
9. Self-control

Please see the operating manual, the B.I.B.L.E. (Believers' Instructions Before Leaving Earth) for further details on the use of these fixes.

WARNING: Continuing to operate the human being unit without correction voids any manufacturer warranties, exposing the unit to dangers and problems too numerous to list and will result in the human unit being permanently impounded. For free emergency service, call on Jesus.

DANGER: The human being units not responding to this recall action will have to be scrapped in the furnace. The SIN defect will not be permitted to enter heaven so as to prevent contamination of that facility. Thank you for your attention!

–God

P.S. You may contact the Father any time by "knee mail." Because He lives!

"Our hope is grounded in the trustworthy character of a God who loves us with an everlasting love." *–Bill Crowder*

~ 80 ~

Romans: 8:24 (KJV) – "But hope that is seen is not hope. [We don't hope for what we already have]."

Paul writes about an important dimension in our study of hope, "Once hope is grasped, it is no longer needed." Whatever we are hoping for becomes real now! We move on to another level of spiritual growth. Salvation is the starting point saved by hope, but then there are other avenues demanding hope.

For instance, Paul uses the analogy of adoption. Without Christ we are orphans, lost in a life without God and without hope. Once we are adopted into the family of God, we become a child of God and have the same inheritance that Jesus has, and we can call God "Daddy" (Abba). Friends who adopted their son always said they chose him; other families had to take what they got with their biological children. But being an heir, being adopted into the family, we now have additional areas of hope, new expectations of success. Adoption is actually a legal term given spiritual meaning—as believers we have been given the full privileges of sonship in the family of God. Wow! And what an inheritance!

Another instance of hope is for the future, an event promised by Jesus. A few years ago, a good friend, Blanche Osborn, wrote a song entitled, "His Next Great Act of Love." At the first performance of the new composition, we tried to imagine the direction she would take us for His next great act. First act, His birth; then, His ministry of preaching and healing; third, His death for our sins, His resurrection from the dead, His ascension. It is the second coming—our Lord's return—His next great act of love.

Blanche helped us focus on hope that is not seen. Since the early church, Christians have been waiting with anticipation for a hope we do not yet have. Many songwriters have tried to convey this hope. As a child, I sang "Coming Again" with little knowledge of what that meant. Bill and Gloria Gaither also inspired a generation of vocalists and worshipers with the thrilling "The King Is Coming." It concludes with the words "Praise God He's coming for me." Now that is hope, expectation of future success.

In his letter to Rome, Paul talks about the "suffering of their present age," but he also says, "All things work together for those that love the Lord to those who are called according to His purpose." That kind of thinking can only come from hope. And, of course, our greatest hope is His next great act of love—His return.

> "His purpose will ripen fast, unfolding every hour, the bud may have a bitter taste, but sweet will be the flower." *—William Cowper*

~ 81 ~

Romans 8:24 (KJV) – *"We are saved by hope."*

The first eight chapters of Paul's letter to the church of Rome contain many popular verses of Scripture. For instance, 8:18 reads, "I reckon that the sufferings of this present time are not to be compared with the glory that shall be revealed in us." And of course they often repeated Romans 8:28, "We know that all things work together for good to those that love God and are called according to His purpose." Nestled between these two are two verses that we will look at the next two days. This letter had a great impact upon two giants of the church, Luther and Wesley.

Long before modern communication methods, the letter was Paul's method of keeping in touch with and instructing believers. There are many in the Christian community who believe this was Paul's clearest and most detailed explanation of the gospel. Is it any wonder, then, that he relates "hope" to salvation? In your mind, underline the word salvation. Tantamount to an understanding of the gospel is an understanding of salvation. Paul could write verses 18 and 28 because his hope was rooted in his salvation.

Occasionally when you mention salvation, there are those who say, "I think I'm saved," or, "I'm not sure." These same people will know if they are married or single, if they are Caucasian or Oriental, Democrats or Republicans, but are confused about their salvation. Simply speaking, we are saved when we accept Christ as our personal Savior (wherever or however that took place). Some have done it at evangelistic services or at their baptism, some as the result of a confirmation course, some during a time of spiritual crisis. The important thing is that we know we have made that acceptance. Then we can say with Paul we are saved by (or in) this hope!

Years ago I preached a simplistic message on salvation. I called it the "ABCs of the Gospel." Obviously, it was not original with me, but it clearly outlined three key steps: ACCEPT the fact we need Jesus as our Savior, BELIEVE He died for me, CONFESS my sins (areas where we have fallen short), and COMMIT our life to Jesus. If you haven't done this yet, this could be a hope-filled day, following the ABCs.

Hope allows us to work to bring God's reign upon the earth – even when we see no results.

> "Our hope begins and ends in God, the source of all hope." *–Mary Lou Redding*

~ 82 ~

Romans 8:25 – *"We hope with perseverance patience . . . wait for it."*

The prayer of ADD personalities and often hyper Christians, "Lord, give me patience and hurry up!" There must have been some of that among the Christians at Rome. Paul had to address such impatience in his letter. Today we would be less than honest if we did not admit an amount of impatience in our religious life. I'm glad that the NKJV (New King James Version of the Bible) uses the word perseverance instead of patience. Perseverance carries with it the additional dimension of endurance.

Today let's think about Paul's life and how much he had to endure. If you want to find a role model for perseverance (patience), choose Paul. In seminary we had a quote about Norman Vincent Peale, comparing him with Paul. The supposition was that Peale was very positive and Paul rather negative in his teaching. Here is the oft-used quote: "Some find Peale appealing and Paul appalling; others find Paul appealing and Peale appalling." I found neither man appalling but appealing in their ministries, but Paul superseded any life lived for Christ. For all the challenges and suffering he confronted, Paul persevered; he endured!

If you think you aren't good enough, the next time you feel like God can't use you, just remember: Noah, at one time, drank too much. Abraham was too old. Isaac was a daydreamer. Jacob was a liar. Leah was unattractive. Joseph was abused. Moses had a stuttering problem. Gideon was afraid. Sampson was a womanizer. Rahab was a prostitute. Jeremiah and Timothy were too young. David had an affair and was a murderer. Elijah was suicidal. Jonah ran from God. Job went bankrupt. John the Baptist ate bugs. Peter denied Christ. The disciples fell asleep while praying. Martha worried about everything. The Samaritan woman was divorced, more than once. Zacchaeus was too small. Paul was too religious. Timothy had an ulcer, and Lazarus was dead!

What do you have that's worse than that? So no more excuses! God can use you to your full potential. Besides, you aren't the message, you are just the messenger. Notice these words of Paul as he continues in the 8th chapter, verse 35:

"Who shall separate us from the love of Christ? Shall trouble or hardship or persecution or famine or nakedness or danger or sword? No, in all these things we are more than conquerors through him that loved us. For I am convinced that neither death nor life, angels or demons, the present or the future, nor any powers, neither height or depth, nor anything else in all creation, will be able to separate us from the love of God that is in Christ Jesus our Lord."

Hope today will do that for us, too. Take the word from the

written page. Look at them! Just four letters—H-O-P-E—and reorder the verse. We will use this acronym: HELPING OUR-SELVES PERSEVERE EVERY DAY. Persevere with patience.

~ 83 ~

Romans 12:12 (NIV) – *"Be joyful in hope, patient in af-fliction, faithful in prayer."*

Those of you who enjoy statistics will be interested to know there are ninety-five references to hope in the Old Testament and eighty-five in the New Testament. Most of those are recorded in this devotional book. I am convinced that our Lord has placed these many Scriptures in His Word to cover all the circumstances and experiences of our life. Today we want to concentrate on what (to quote a contemporary cliché) turns you on. Or maybe we could ask, "What gets me excited?"

Most of my friends and my entire family are into sports. Whether on a professional level, college, high school, or sand lot level, we take winning and losing seriously. The term fanatic is derived from "fan," and we are fans of our local teams to the point of being fanatical. There is nothing like victory for excitement and nothing like defeat for a downer. As I look at my spiritual life and compare it with sports, I pray, "Lord help me to get as excited over the work of the kingdom as I do the Phillies winning the World Series."

Bill and Gloria Gaither were aware of this when a few years ago they wrote a song, "Get All Excited." The lyrics are a challenge to all of us. In it they encourage Christians to tell others about the gospel. The message is to keep the main thing the main thing. Get excited about what can really bring us joy —HOPE, expectation of success. Be turned on to hope so that we can be patient in affliction and faithful in prayer.

As a child, the gifts of Christmas or a birthday were exciting. Now as we mature in our walk with God, we are excited about the gifts of Jesus as a personal Savior. As adults we are excited about marriage, our first child, our education, our first home, our occupation. Now it is time to grow up and get excited about how God is working in our life and to seek first the kingdom of God and His righteousness. Be a "fan" for Jesus today—a blessed fanatic for the king of kings.

"Hope is a good thing, maybe the best of things." *–From the film: The Shawshank Redemption*

~ 84 ~

Romans 15:4 (NKJV) – *"Whatever things were written before were written for our learning, that we might have hope."*

Most of our learning comes from what has been previously written. I remember pulling up behind a car with an interesting bumper sticker. At first I thought it was a familiar quote often placed for easy reading, but this one surprised me. "If you can read this, you're too close." No, that was what I was expecting. Rather it read, "If you can read this, thank a teacher!" Thank a teacher. In fact, as you read this, thank a teacher. And especially a Sunday school teacher.

Paul knew there was much written before his letter that had already influenced his readers. Every Jewish child was well schooled in the Scriptures of their day. They knew well the commandments, the Law, the history of their people and, of course, their great heroes of the faith. Paul was "learned" in his Jewish heritage and states here that one of its purposes was to give hope.

So today's study reminds us of our indebtedness to those before us who taught so we could learn about hope. Focus for a moment on teachers, ministers, parents, and friends who gave us the foundational knowledge of Jesus. We did not come into this world with a computer chip in our brain filled with all the teachings of the gospel.

I have a sermon entitled "All I Need to Know I Learned in Sunday School." (No apologies to an author who wrote *All I Need to Know I Learned in Kindergarten*.) I learned that God is the Creator, Jesus is the Savior. A book called *God's Word, the Bible,* is my guidebook. I learned a song, "Jesus Loves the Little Children." That song helped me with race relations—red and yellow, black and white, they are all precious in His sight. Jesus loves the little children of the world." I learned that one day I will die and go to live with God.

We can make our own bumper sticker. Is it your experience that you owe much to a Sunday school teacher? Did they teach you the basic stories of the Bible, your first gospel songs, and the importance of Jesus in your life? If so, make that bumper sticker.

Prayer: "Father, you are my strength and the origin of my hope. Thank you for teachers that taught me your

Word and helped me in my formative years to have an expectation of success. Amen."

~ 85 ~

Romans 15:13 (NIV) – "May the God of hope fill you with joy and peace as you trust in him, so you may overflow with hope."

The opening verse of the fifteenth chapter of Romans is the foundation of our ministry at Ranch Hope. "We that are strong [that know the Lord] ought to bear with the failings of those who are weak and not to please ourselves." As I drive into our campus, those words often greet me, as they are posted on the sign board at the entrance to our campus. Our ministry to troubled youth has been bringing hope (expectation of success) to thousands of young people since our inception, because we are not here to please ourselves, but to overflow with hope.

Paul's imagery of our life overflowing with hope needs to be amplified today. It is one thing to have hope from the God of hope; it is still even more to be overflowing with hope. In one translation, the word overflowing reads abounding.

Ever see waves abounding at the seashore? It means they just keep coming, one wave after another endlessly. Like the song "Sailing, sailing, over the bounding main," the God of hope just brings hope coming to us endlessly as we trust in Him and are filled by the power of His Holy Spirit. So today sit with me at the seashore. Look out at the ocean, then focus on the shore—watching the waves abound and overflowing with hope.

The "New" Footprints

Now imagine you and the Lord Jesus are walking along the beach together. For much of the way, the Lord's footprints go along steadily, consistently, rarely varying in the pace. But your prints are in a disorganized stream of zigzags, starts, stops, turn-arounds, circles, departures, and returns. For much of the way it seems to go like this. But gradually, your footprints come in line with the Lord's, soon paralleling His consistently. You and Jesus are walking as true friends.

This seems perfect, but then an interesting thing happens: Your footprints that once etched the sand next to the Master's are now walking precisely in His steps. Inside His large footprints is the smaller "sand print," safely enclosed. You and Jesus are becoming one; this goes on for many miles.

But gradually you notice another change. The footprints insider the larger footprints seem to grow larger. Eventually they disappear altogether. There is only one set of footprints. They have become one! Again this goes on for a long time.

Then something awful happens. The second set of footprints is back. This time it seems even worse than before. Zigzags all over the place. Stop, start, deep gashes in the sand. A veritable mess of prints. You're amazed and shocked. But this is the end of your dream.

Now you speak, "Lord, I understand the first scene with the zigzags, fits, starts, and so on. I was a new Christian, just learning. But You walked on through the storm and helped me learn to walk with You."

"That is correct," replies the Lord.

"Then when the smaller footprints were inside of Yours, I was actually learning to walk in Your steps. I followed You very closely."

"Very good. You have understood everything so far."

"Then the smaller footprints grew and eventually filled in with Yours. I suppose that I was actually growing so much that I was becoming more like You in every way."

"Precisely."

"But this is my question, Lord. Was there a regression or something? The footprints went back to two, and this time it was worse than the first."

The Lord smiles, then laughs. "You didn't know? That was when we danced!"

For He will turn your mourning into dancing! –Psalm 30:11

"Dear Lord, Give me hope. My boat is so small, and the ocean is so great!" *–Seaman's prayer*

~ 86 ~

1 Corinthians 9:10 – *"When the plowman plows and the thresher threshes, they ought to do so in sharing the harvest."*

Growing up in southern New Jersey, I have been surrounded by farmland all my life. New Jersey is still called the Garden State, and we believe (in the south) we are the garden spot of the garden state. South Jersey farmers have to live by hope. A.W. Tozer said it well when he wrote, "Miracles follow the plow." Watching farmers plow the soil, plant the seed, fertilize, and irrigate, I knew they were working hard for future harvests. They were laboring with expectation that miracles would follow their plow.

In this verse, Paul is writing as one who also grew up in an agrarian society. He, too, was surrounded by farms and farmers. The people of his day could easily relate to this analogy of the plow plowing and the thrasher thrashing. And Paul wants them to know that he is an apostle who is doing his job and should be compensated. But he also wants the receiver of his letter in Corinth to know he would never take advantage of his position in Christ. "All who work in the field will share the harvest." This verse precedes his often quoted phrase, "Woe unto me if I do not preach the Gospel."

In our local church, on the mission field, or in our family we may not see the results of our plowing and planting. But remember, Jesus said, "No man, having put his hand to the plow, and looking back, is fit for the kingdom of God" (Luke 9:62). Hope says, "Don't look back; keep looking ahead to the harvest." In Jesus' parable of the wheat and tare, He illustrates how it is difficult to complete the cycle of plowing, planting, and harvesting.

The enemy (the devil) plants tares (weeds) in the garden, attempting to destroy the good wheat. Have you ever noticed we do not have to plant weeds? I never go to the local garden mart and ask for a bag of weeds. In this parable the problem is magnified because tares look like wheat. To the casual observer, they look the same. Jesus says the workers were not permitted to start pulling up the tares because they might destroy good wheat by mistake. The farmer tells his helpers, "Let them grow together, until the harvest." Jesus reminds us that in the end the wheat wins. The wheat is gathered into the barn, and the tares are burned up. So today keep plowing and planting; miracles will follow.

> "Our hope is to grow stronger and taller as our roots dig deeper in the soft soil along the banks of the river of life." *–Chuck Swindoll*

~ 87 ~

1 Corinthians 13:13 (NKJV) – *"And now abide faith, hope, love."*

Today's hope verse is possibly the most often-quoted passage from Paul's letters. Read at weddings for the bride and groom to focus on, it is an eternal trilogy that will be the foundation of their marriage. But Paul was not speaking of romantic (erotic) love. Here he is referring to agape love. Agape love is the highest form of love taught by the Christian faith—loving the unlovable, the loveless, those that can't or won't love us back.

The church at Corinth was filled with factions and fighting. Division and separation were the M.O. of the Christians in Corinth. It was the church to write a letter to about faith, hope, and love. Remember, it was a young church and very vulnerable to every spiritual disease and disorder. After starting this church in ancient Greece, Paul found, just two years later, spiritual arrogance, sexual promiscuity, abuse of spiritual gifts, and ignorance of basic Christian teaching. This letter addresses all these issues with FAITH, HOPE, and LOVE.

Nestled between faith (trust) and love is the word hope. What a threesome to incorporate in our life today. First we have faith in God, we trust Him, then we place our hope in Him (our expectation of success), and finally we love God by living out agape love. Of course, Paul adds the additional teaching "and the greatest of these is love." Comparatively speaking, love trumps the other two but does not negate them. In fact, we could say hope is one of the stepping stones to love.

In high school, my life was dramatically changed when Eileen Brown moved to my hometown. It was my senior year, and that summer her family relocated because of her father's work as a boilermaker. How unfortunate for Eileen that in her senior year she had to change schools, but a blessing for me. Having seen the "new girl in town," my greatest hope was to meet her and, of course, go out on a date. That was sixty years ago. From faith in my ability to woo her, to hope that she would respond, we fell in love and were married in my senior year of college. This is a simplistic illustration of how our Lord can work through faith, hope, and love on a daily basis in our lives.

"Without hope, everything I nailed down is coming loose." *–Anonymous*

~ 88 ~

1 Corinthians 15:19 (KJV) – *"If in this life only we have hope in Christ, we are of all men most miserable."*

The resurrection of each of us personally is a future event. It, therefore, is our most challenging "expectation of success." Paul, writing to the Church at Corinth, puts hope in an important perspective for us. Hope is not limited to our experience on earth. In fact, Paul makes it clear that if hope is confined to our journey on planet earth, we will be miserable. Death waits for us in the future with all its finality and grief.

There are many in our culture, religious and nonreligious, who will concede that the gospel of Jesus Christ presents a great way to live. His teachings, eliminating the miracles and eternal life, provide a great framework for "the good life." How often have you heard the expression, "Just keeping the Golden Rule" will certainly change the world? It is difficult to argue with that, but it misses a dimension of Jesus' teaching that far exceeds temporal concerns.

Imagine before your birth in your mother's womb, you were a twin. Your twin says, "Our nine months are up; we're moving out." Both of you had spent the past nine months since conception "hooked up" to your mother. You were safe and sound—warm, comfortable, being fed—and now you are told you are going to leave this environment. There would be many elements of fear and concern if you were able to comprehend this change. "We're going into a wonderful new world," your twin would try to encourage you. "There is something more beyond the womb." To say the least, we would be skeptical.

Jesus told us there is something more beyond the tomb. However many years we spend here on earth is our human existence; it will come to an end. Jesus came to tell us that there is more beyond this, and Paul amplified this in his teachings. We

have hope—expectations of a future beyond death—resurrection! Avoid misery. Don't limit the gospel, the life in Christ, to one dimension.

> "When facing illness or tragedy, I want to feel His great compassion and faithfulness. I want to know His great hope and wealth."

~ 89 ~

2 Corinthians 1:7 (NIV) – *"And our hope for you is firm, because we know that just as you share in our sufferings, so also you share in our comfort."*

My Bible has a bold, black capital heading over this portion of Scripture: Comfort in suffering. I am blessed by the word IN; it carries a message by itself. Actually, I would rather see the word FROM—that would be more palatable—comfort FROM suffering. A world of difference exists between these two prepositions. But Paul makes it very clear in this second letter to the Christians of Corinth that they will suffer just as Christ suffered. Suffering is our link to Christ. Many have written about this, and it would be good for us to review their thoughts.

- C.S. Lewis, in his book *The Problem of Pain* said, "You would like to know how I behave when I am experiencing pain, not writing books about it. You need not guess, for I will tell you, I am a great coward . . . But what is the good of telling you about my feelings? They are the same as yours . . . pain hurts!"

- Martin Luther said, "Were it not for tribulation, I should not understand Scripture."

- Joni Eareckson Tada, paralyzed as a teenager in a diving accident, wrote in the book Joni, "My own fiery trials were now a little easier to cope with and I saw how I fit in with God's scheme of things, especially through reading the Word . . . the word from Psalms [41:3] became personal to me 'The Lord will sustain (me) on (my) sickbed.'"

- Corrie ten Boom, prisoner in the Nazi concentration camp Ravensbruck, wrote these words after her release: "I do not understand the 'why' of suffering, except my own suffering in this place, God brought me here for a specific task. I was here to lead the sorrowing and despairing to the Savior... I was to point the way to heaven to people, many whom were soon to die." The "why" of my suffering was no problem to me.

• Hope for Paul is built on that firm conviction that all who share in Christ's suffering will also share in His comfort. There is an often-quoted phrase: "Jesus came to comfort the afflicted and afflict the comfortable," with the emphasis on the latter. Today we will emphasize the former, comfort the afflicted. Our hope is built on the Savior who comforts us when we share in His suffering.

In closing this section, focus with me on the words of Jesus, "Those who would come after me must deny themselves, take up the cross, and follow me." Like Dietrich Bonhoeffer, martyred German pastor, I believe this outlines the cost of Christian discipleship. Paul would also know these words and teach them to the Christians in Corinth. Comfort is shared by those who put Christ first and self second, and take up the cross of love for God and people and follow Jesus.

> Prayer: "I come to you, Lord, because you habitually give hope to the hopeless and rest to the weary. Encourage us today as we struggle with life. In Jesus' name, amen."

~ 90 ~

2 Corinthians 1:10 (NIV) – *"On Him have we set our hope that He will continue to deliver us."*

As Paul opens his second letter to the church at Corinth, there are some who believe he is offering up complaints to God. Paul uses words like troubles, sufferings, distress, hardship, great pressure, despair, and the sentence of death. But upon a close reading of these verses, we see just the opposite. He is not complaining but making it clear that his hardships would bring glory to God. Maybe you can make a list (long or short) of challenges you have been faced with lately. Go ahead, write them down. Then pray over each one and learn what Paul learned, "We set our hope on God and he will continue to deliver us."

Have you ever heard of Ed Dobson? You can learn a great deal about him and his dealings with adversities by going online to edsstory.com. Briefly, here is an outline of this man's struggles and his victory through hope: Ed was diagnosed with ALS (Lou Gehrig's disease). He was given only two to five years to live. I have watched two close friends die of this horrible physical disorder. The body shuts down muscle by muscle, organ by organ, and death is horrendous. Ed has now lived ten years since the diagnosis. He has used this time to wrestle with issues that suffering raises—identity, worry, forgiveness, gratitude, and healing. During these years he has centered on making films to encourage others. A quote from his seven-part film series sums it up, "Emerging from it all is his discovery that there is always hope."

Today what are we set on? We are blessed by medical science and the art of healing. We are blessed by the fields of social sciences and psychological therapy. We are blessed by a world of "goodies," with its many gadgets and abundance of material things. Yet we find ourselves more and more in need of the hope that men like Ed Dobson has found. Reread Paul's list of events that could have destroyed the average person. But he would write—later in this opening chapter—"We might not rely on ourselves but on God who raises the dead." The focus of our life, to be hopeful, is on the DEAD RAISER.

"Hope, like faith, and a purpose in life is medicinal. Hope is both biological and psychologically vital to mankind." *–Dr. Harold Wolfe*

~ 91 ~

2 Corinthians 3:12 – *"Seeing that we have such hope we are bold."*

Hope and boldness! Hope can make us bold. Paul wants the Corinthian Christians to have freedom of speech, to be open in their witness for Christ, to be frank, to be courageous. Easier said than done. Every generation of Christians has had to deal with a certain timidity and reluctance sharing our hope. But Paul certainly gave us an example to follow.

Years ago I attended a county fair. It was the old-fashioned type with 4-H competitions, cooking and preserving contests, tractor pulls, a small midway, and plenty of people. We thought it would be a great opportunity to reach people with Christ's message. Our gospel group called "The Hopefuls" would sing and attract a crowd, then we would witness to our faith. It all sounded great until the actual night and seeing the actual crowds. We sang and the people gathered, but then the boldness—the courage, the freshness to speak—well, to say the least it took a long time coming.

One man stood out in the crowd. He shouted, "Go home. We're

here to have fun. Keep your religion in church!" My only hope was that we could pack up and go home. But God had other plans. After each song and each time of testimony, we grew stronger and more people listened. I felt at times like Paul in the marketplace of Athens, or John Wesley in the coal mines of England. But hope made us more and more bold. We were not able to tabulate "decisions for Christ" that night at the fair or whether we had any impact on people lives, but something happened to all of us. Our singing and sharing made each of us stronger in our faith.

Do you personally find it difficult to be bold in your faith? Please note that boldness does not make us arrogant or irritating to those we witness. It is the greatest act of love to share with someone the hope that is in us. I've often thought, as we are critical of people like Jehovah's Witnesses, it would be great to see more Christian witnesses (Methodist witnesses, Baptist witnesses, etc.). Begin today to seek ways and means to have the hope that makes us bold.

> "True hope responds to the real world, to real life; it is an active effort." *—Walter Anderson*

~ 92 ~

2 Corinthians 7:13 – *"By this we have hope."*

Have you ever received a critical letter, for example, correspondence from someone who disagreed with you on some issue and decided to pen the grievance? I used to keep such letters (enough of them to keep me humble) and would periodically review the written concerns. In most cases I would respond and try to address each issue raised by the critics. The apostle Paul has written such an epistle, or "severe letter" as he calls it, to the Church of Corinth. It is a critique of the Corinthians and some of their lifestyles. Reading 2 Corinthians 6 and 7, we see first-hand his grievance against the church.

But Paul has written this negative message for positive results. And it worked! Note verse 9: "For you were made sorry in a godly manner and your sorrow led to repentance." Having a critical spirit for the sake of being critical is not the goal of any Christian; being critical to help one's spiritual growth is important. Many of the letters I kept over the years did not help my growth as a believer. Some were downright nasty and written in order to hurt; eventually they ended up being shredded. I can remember one letter in particular that asked me, "How did you get in this racket?" In reviewing the letter, I realized the writer was very critical of our ministry on the radio and also to youth. In a sense he was saying we were in it only for the money. Oddly enough, he shocked me by including a generous gift and writing, "This is for the kids and not for you." I can take that kind of criticism as long as the critic wants to help a troubled child.

However, legitimate criticism helped me in my spiritual journey. There have been those who challenged me to avoid taking credit for God's blessing and grace in growing Ranch Hope. When someone helps you to stay focused, you should praise the Lord. But notice today, in addition to the letter Paul sends Titus to represent him, now there was a touch of genius. It is one thing to write a message; it is another to send a representative to reinforce the message. On one occasion when a state worker wanted to know what we were doing with the youth he had sent us, we let him speak directly with the young people, and he saw the change in them. For the apostle Paul, Titus has been referred to as a "point man," a pinch hitter, a clutch player, all because he knew how to deal with dangerous and unpopular situations. Paul started a church in Crete and then left Titus in charge. Thus Paul knew he could trust Titus to bring leadership and calm to Corinth. All of us sometime or the other needs a critique of our spiritual life. We need to "repent" when necessary and then move on.

Today's verse of Scripture not only tells us of hope (comfort or encouragement), it also speaks of the joy that the Christians have found in the visit of Titus. Hope comes from a visitation sent on a special assignment from Paul, and notice Titus's visit brought JOY, and he also has his spirit refreshed.

"In every loss, God offers hope."   *–F. Richard Garland*

~ 93 ~

2 Corinthians 10:15 (KJV) – *"Not boasting . . . of other men's labours; but having hope, when your faith is increased, that we shall be enlarged by you."*

From prison Paul sends a message of hope to the church at Corinth. As his message is written, I'm sure he could visualize the city where he had first preached the gospel to the brand new mission field. People that he had led to Christ were now leaders in this church. But of course they needed additional leadership from their mentor and spiritual authority. However, there were changes taking place, and some were beginning to question Paul's leadership and authority.

They—all of us have run into them. They don't like your appearance. They think you are _____ _____ (fill in the blank). They question your motives. They, they, they. A good question is, who are they? In Paul's case, they were Christians who measured themselves by themselves, by their own opinion of themselves. (How convenient.) Paul, on the other hand, worked on the basic premise, "Be sure others are more important than yourself."

Yet in these circumstances and under this duress, Paul wants the church to look beyond personal boasting. Hope (expectation of success) will be of our faith increasing and that even more mission fields will hear the gospel. Personal gain is not the issue; sharing the good news of Jesus is. Remember the story that is told in the book of Acts about Paul's vision of a man from Macedonia? Paul is awakened from his sleep and is called to start a new church in this fabled land. I have used an acronym to outline what Paul was able to accomplish in Macedonia.

M – Ministry
I – Instruction
S – Service
S – Spiritual help
I – Important
O – Opportunity
N – Now

As you can see, this acronym spells mission. Paul, throughout his walk with Christ, was on a mission.

Years ago, at a national convention, I collected a number of business cards. They were all quite creative and gave the necessary details about a ministry. Everything was included, from name, title of position, e-mail, phone and mailing address, etc. But one card grabbed my attention. Instead of just INC (incorporated), it read INC "in the name of Christ." I hope that was more than a gimmick to get my attention. Looking at it, I thought about Ranch Hope for Boys and Girls, Inc. (in the name of Christ). Sometimes business cards can be a way of boasting. Hope brings the success of our ministry into focus. It must always be about the Lord Jesus and His gospel.

"The good news is this: every struggle has within it a seed of hope." *—F. Richard Garland*

~ 94 ~

Galatians 5:5 (KJV) – *"For we through the Spirit wait for the hope of righteousness by faith.*

The hope of right living—we eagerly wait for it. There is expectation of success because we live holy lives. In this study, hope is the result of living the right kind of life. Paul had to address this issue at this time because in Galatia there were differing interpretations of the gospel. The old struggle of legalism and grace was raising its ugly head. Paul had to stand against the legalist and outline the differences between grace and law.

You may want to read Paul's contrast between two covenants with God—one represented by Abraham's son Isaac, and the other by his son Ishmael. For Paul, Isaac was born of the spirit, Ishmael of the flesh; Isaac was born of Abraham's wife Sarah, and Ishmael born of the bondwoman Hagar. Abraham and Sarah tried to have a child in their own strength, but eventually God's promise was fulfilled miraculously in the birth of Isaac. Paul wanted the Christians of Galatians to avoid even the emphasis on circumcision, because this, too, led the believer right back to the law instead of to the new liberty in Christ, liberty to do the "right thing."

The battle still rages. The church is often divided on what is right living. There was a time when the major emphasis of some churches was "not to smoke, not to chew, and not to go with boys that do." A Nazarene friend of mine tells me of his youth when girls and boys could not swim on the same beach together. Even the Amish and Mennonites have had to struggle with law and grace—only black and grey carriages, or only black cars with no chrome bumpers? But for us today our hope is based on what we do, not what we don't do. We have the liberty to live for God.

One author has said we have formed imperfect freedom:

Freedom to make money – For the Christians we then pray for the grace to know how to use money.

Freedom to be known –Freedom to make a name for ourselves in some capacity. Then we use the position to glorify God.

Freedom to be a leader – There are leaders and followers. As a leader we have the responsibility to lead others with the skills God has given us.

And having freedom for pleasure – each freedom gives us an opportunity to spread hope through righteous living.

"Everything that is done in the world is done by hope."
–*Martin Luther*

~ 95 ~

Ephesians 1:11–12 (NIV) – *"In Him we were also chosen, having been predestined according to the plan of Him who works out everything in conformity with the purpose of his will, in order that we, who were the first to put our hope in Christ, might be for the praise of His glory."*

You probably will have to read the Scripture again. This is the longest and most controversial teaching we have studied on hope. It would be easy to gloss over this passage, but it contains important truth for both Calvinists and Armenians (e.g. Presbyterians and Methodists). Without making this chapter a minicourse on Christian theology (check the Internet or your bookstore for that), there is still much to give us an expectation of success.

The question is often asked, "If God chooses us, do we have any choice?" Roger Olson, writing in Christianity Today, tells the story of a gospel tract that he handed out in his neighborhood as a young boy. It was based upon a sermon preached by Herschel Hobbs, called "God's Election Day." The devil and God had an election to determine whether you would be lost or saved. The devil voted against you and the Lord voted for you. So the vote was a tie. It was up to you to cast the deciding vote.

Most popular theology would probably agree with that analogy, but of course there would be those who would totally disagree. Let me briefly outline differing schools of thought.

Some believe our salvation is limited completely to God's sovereign grace. Unless God appointed you for salvation, you are lost. God chooses us before we respond to Him. God's mercy is foremost, not our effort. Others just as strongly believe that God gives everyone the ability and opportunity to choose. Each individual has to respond—repent of sin and turn to Christ. We can either accept or reject salvation.

But for today's verse on hope, both approaches are important. Why? Because that first generation of Christians did not get bogged down in theology. They were the first to hope in Christ. What a privilege—the FIRST. What a responsibility—the first to bring hope, long before John Calvin or Jacob Arminius. Paul was dealing with questions like, "Why am I here; what am I to do while here; and where do I go when it is all over?" For Paul, hope had to do with making peace with God, identifying with Christ and getting prepared for eternity. And remember he wrote this letter from prison.

"Life finds a way." *–Jurassic Park movie*

"God has a better way—hope." *–Dave Bailey*

~ 96 ~

Ephesians 1:18 (NKJV) – *"That you may know what is the hope of His calling."*

Ephesus was the capital of the Roman province of Asia. Today it would be considered a part of Turkey. The church there was started by Paul and was the center of missionary and evangelistic outreach to the rest of Asia. You may remember that this is the city where those who made idols to Diana and other gods rioted because the gospel was negatively affecting their businesses. People who come to Christ turned from idols made by human hands.

Paul writes this letter from prison (at least house arrest), and today's verse is a part of his teaching in spiritual wisdom. Hope is predicated on wisdom (not wishful thinking). He wants our eyes opened to divine truth, not just human knowledge—the hope of His calling. It is in Jesus that we find true hope; all other wisdom is limited, as were the idols made by human hands.

Our world is impressed by academic degrees and human knowledge. We hear it over and over again: "education" is our salvation. One wise sage, however, sarcastically said, "Take a dumb devil, send him to college, then you may get a smart devil." Having spent nearly twelve years on college and university campuses for three degrees, I can attest to education's limits in transforming a society. Our nation is filled with colleges, universities, community colleges, high schools, trade schools, etc. And still we struggle with direction and hope. Today we read in horror about the assaults on American young people in our schools. There are many who raise the question, "Is this the result of a more secular society that has eliminated prayer, reference to the Bible, study of our religious roots, and moral teachings?" Only time will tell, but our hope is that our academic institutions will also see that the hope of their calling is in the Lord.

Maybe we need to get rid of the idols as they did in Ephesus. Paul would encourage us today to "know the hope of His calling." My first college was founded by Methodist pastors to "lead out" (educate) college young people from darkness to light. That was the basis of education. The open Bible was on the logo to help those students find hope in the truth of the gospel. Now, years later, the college has changed. Like many colleges and other organizations founded by Christian groups, time brings changes. Often the Word of God is no longer the centerpiece of education and Christ no longer the foundation. New idols had promised a new hope for a new generation.

"Learn from yesterday, live for today, hope for tomorrow." *–Albert Einstein*

~ 97 ~

Ephesians 2:12 (NKJV) – *"At that time you were without Christ, being aliens from the commonwealth of Israel and strangers from the covenants of promise, having no hope and without God in the world."*

If you were an artist, you couldn't paint a better word picture of how bleak it is to be without Christ. Paul, in these few words to the church of Ephesus, gives a portrait of those he calls "aliens." We usually think of aliens in terms of creatures from a foreign planet, but Paul states this is our condition before knowing Christ. Spiritually, we are from another planet—alienated from God with no hope.

We all know or have known people who are hopeless. Our TV and computer screen, newspapers, and other media portray a world in need of HOPE. Most of the world's leadership—political, social, academic, and military—do no share Paul's belief that the root cause is Christlessness. Christ can make us hopeful; there is hope in Him. Paul would echo the words of the hymn, "On Christ the solid rock I stand, all other ground is sinking sand. All other ground is sinking sand."

Can you remember when you were still an alien? No, not the one who entered our nation illegally, but when you were still without Christ. You may have been like me—raised in the church, active in Sunday school, sang in the choir, a leader of my youth group, confirmed at age twelve, christened as an infant—but still an alien. Why? Because it was all about me. That's right, I was in the church but still lost in the world, and in Paul's words an alien.

"Instead of giving me reason why I can't, hope gives me reason why I can." *−Anonymous*

~ 98 ~

Ephesians 4:4–6 (NIV) – *"There is one body and one Spirit, just as you were called to one hope when you were called; one Lord, one faith, one baptism; one God and Father of all."*

Today's hope is based on the ONE. Note how many times the word one is used by the apostle Paul (seven) writing to the church at Ephesus. The word hope is tied in with one—one hope of our calling. By dictionary definition, one means union, harmony, agreement, accord, a single purpose, rather than division or separation.

All of us know from experience, however, that there are divisions in the church. As Christians we are often separated with our various interpretations of the Scriptures, theology, and church history. That is probably why Paul wants to remind us there is a "hope of one calling" that must supersede differences. I have learned over the years of ministry that there can be diversity and still oneness.

I have ministered in revival services, Bible studies, retreats, youth camps, and talks on Ranch Hope in many different denominations. The "oneness" of our faith in Christ always outweighs our differences. My "one hope of my calling" took me to Friends Meeting Houses, Pentecostal, Methodist, Baptist, Presbyterian, and Nazarene churches—even drinking wine and preaching at Catholic and Episcopal Churches during Lent or other "holy days," conducting and assisting in weddings and funerals, always emphasizing our ONENESS in spirit. As one writer said, "Two Christians are better than one, when they're one."

Here is a challenge for today's "expectation of success." Surely in your family, your church, your workplace, school, wherever there are Christians who are "different" from you, make it a point of prayer to draw a circle that brings them in, not shuts them out. Find ways to emphasize "one body, one Spirit, one Lord, one faith, one baptism, one God—and one HOPE for our calling." Then ONE will not be the loneliest number that you'll ever know.

> "Love recognizes no barriers. It jumps hurdles, leaps fences, penetrates walls to arrive at its destination full of hope." *–Maya Angelou*

~ **99** ~

Philippians 1:19–20 (NKJV) – *"For I know that this will turn out for my deliverance through your prayer and the supply of the Spirit of Jesus Christ, according to my earnest expectation and hope."*

Talk about confidence. Paul opens his letter to the Philippians by writing, "I know this will turn out for my deliverance." It reminds me of the words of a song written by Andraé Crouch: "I've got confidence my God will see me through; no matter what the case may be, I know that He will fix it for me."

Remember, Paul is in jail, isolated from the world, in a sewer on death row, and he has confidence. We certainly need that same kind of confidence today. "No matter what the case may be." But notice that Paul calls upon the Christians at Philippi to pray for him. He writes, "I'll be delivered through your prayer." Underline that in your spiritual book and deposit that thought every day. Pray for those who need to be delivered—from persecution, sin, disease, depression, addiction,—the many evils that come against us in life. Never apologize that you can "only pray" for someone. That is our greatest source of life for those struggling and in need of confidence.

This important teaching was dramatically illustrated with a phone call from a Christian woman here in South Jersey. She had called and asked an important question, "What can I do to help the boys and girls of Ranch Hope?" Without hesitation I responded, "First of all, you can pray for us, and secondly you can send some money." There was a long pause on the phone, and she finally responded, "Well, I'll be praying." We have often laughed about that, but I have realized how important prayer warriors are for this ministry. We did need her prayers. By the way, she also became a generous financial contributor.

Of course, Paul is also aware that he needs something in addition to the Philippians' prayer and that is "the supply of the Spirit of Jesus Christ." What a great combination of help—prayer and the work of the Holy Spirit of God. The word supply should bless us, as it is used here. Originally it meant a wealthy person helping meet the costs of musicians or dancers, like benefactors today contribute to the arts. But later it meant any supply of resources that would meet someone's needs. Paul knew that his God "could supply all his needs according to His riches in glory." Once again, that is our formulation of confidence.

Finally, look at the context of hope today. "According to my earnest expectation." This phase used by Paul is actually the translation of a Greek word that means an outstretched hand straining to reach something. The total focus is on the object to be reached, in this case, hope. Paul strained for hope—confidence, expectation of success—in his walk with the Lord, and that is why he can write in verse 21, "For me to live in Christ and even to die is gain." Today reach out for hope, and have the confidence Paul did.

> "He who does not have hope to win has already lost."
> –*Jose Olmedo*

~ 100 ~

Philippians 2:23 (NKJV) – *"Therefore I hope to send him at once, as soon as I see how it goes with me."*

The believers in Philippi needed a message of hope. Paul had just written a disturbing critique about the world Christians lived in, "a wicked and perverted generation." Then on top of that he adds he is "being poured out as a drink offering on the sacrifices and services of your faith." Some interpreted that as a somber message, predicting his own martyrdom. But this was all a prelude to the good news that Paul was hoping to send young Timothy to Philippi.

Timothy was a remarkable young man. Paul considered him his son and had ministered with him for ten years. What a name—Timothy. It means "one who honors God." The name was well chosen by his parents, for as a coworker with Paul, he was deeply respected as one who honored God. It is important to note that his mother, Eunice, and grandmother, Lois, were also believers. Is it any wonder Paul hoped to send Timothy to this young, struggling church as his personal representative? Timothy had been with Paul when the church was founded!

Paul's hope—his expectation of success—was to be a blessing to others. His hope was to send help even if he could not personally be there. You and I have that same opportunity on a daily basis. My wife, Eileen, has a wonderful ministry of sending cards—cards for birthdays, anniversaries, holidays, sympathy, get well, congratulations, encouragement—you name it, she sends it. These cards go all over the world where she can't possibly be, but they are her blessing for the recipients. Other friends we know have ministries of prayer or financial support to missionaries they will never visit, but each prayer, each gift sends hope. But I can't leave this verse without noting Paul's words, "As soon as I see how it goes." This is a reference to Paul's personal condition. He has been in prison and is also suffering from bad health.

That is a tough combination for anyone. So today—now—follow Paul's example. Begin to think of your ministry for hope, how you can bless others, by sending hope in whatever means or method, you will be a Timothy to someone in need.

A prayer for hope: Dear Jesus, I am in a situation where I have little hope. Please forgive me and breathe genuine hope into my life. I surrender my heart to you and ask you to take control of my life. Paul knew prison and physical pain and still kept you first in his life. Help me to do the same. Amen.

~ 101 ~

Colossians 1:5 (NKJV) – *"The hope which is laid up for you in heaven."*

Notice in this opening chapter of the letter to Colossae, Paul uses three terms together: faith (in Jesus Christ), love (for all the saints), and hope (laid up in heaven). The same trilogy is used in 1 Corinthians 13. In this context, the good news of hope is when we practice faith and love here in this life, and the end result is to be with Jesus in heaven.

Often when a new employee is interviewed at Ranch Hope, the question will arise: "Does the Ranch provide any fringe benefit? What is your total financial packet?" Of course, the applicant is referring to health, medical, dental, eyes, and a retirement program. When I was still in that department and talking one on one with the perspective employee, I would jokingly say, "Oh, yes. We have the best retirement program on the planet and then point heavenward." Sometimes they would get it and nervously laugh; other times they would just stare at me like, duh!

Today we can revisit our belief that hope is also our expectation of heaven. Heaven is not just wishful thinking, it is our ultimate destination. You have heard the phrase before, but it is worth repeating. "Heaven is a prepared place for prepared people." Paul says, "Keep faith in Jesus, love our fellow Christians, and expect heaven." Wow, heaven is such a great "fringe benefit." It has been prepared for us, "laid up for us in heaven."

Christian writer Chuck Swindoll was wandering through an old cemetery with his daughter and she became very quiet. Chuck found they both became more and more quiet as they realized they were on holy ground. Chuck was thinking of all those who had passed on that were beneath the ground under those various markers. Then he begun to write down these thoughts: the first one that came to him is life is short. Then he thought, death is sure and wrote that down, and every person born, dies. Third he wrote, opportunity is always now. Those people beneath the sod had no opportunity to come to the Lord, but Chuck and his little daughter had time to serve Him, to love Him, and to know Christ as their personal Savior. Let's keep that in mind—life is short, death is sure, and opportunity is always now. So make the best of it for the Lord today.

"Those who lean on God's love always have reason for hope" –*Joy Gage*

~ 102 ~

Colossians 1:23 (NKJV) – *"If indeed you continue in the faith, grounded and steadfast, and are not moved away from the hope of the gospel you heard."*

Every one of us has had events happen in our lives that could cause us to think of a moving van. Paul was well aware of the temptations and challenges facing a young church at Colossae. In particular, certain members were teaching doctrinal heresies. Of course, there was probably an attempt to bring in Judaism. Some scholars believe there was an emphasis on salvation through works, and a form of mysticism that claimed Jesus was a higher being but not God. Every generation of Christians has had to be reminded to continue in the faith, grounded and steadfast. This gives us the hope of the gospel.

Let's take a moment and park at the word steadfast. Paul writes earlier to the church of Corinth: "Be steadfast, unmovable, always abounding in the work of the Lord." Modern translation of "be steadfast" is "get a grip." Get a grip on things that are really important, and that grip will help us be unmovable. We won't move away from the gospel because we maintain our grip on Jesus.

For years the poster hung in the class room at Strang School on our Ranch Hope campus. You may have seen a similar version at your church. Reread it with me: "If you feel far away from God today, guess who moved." The message is obvious. God never leaves us; we leave God. The message at Strang School is our message of hope today. Paul writes to the Christians at Colossae: Don't move away from the hope of the gospel.

At a Promise Keepers rally in Washington, DC, a few years ago, a speaker said something that I wrote in the margin of my Bible. I did not write his name—for his name was incidental to his challenge. "In our walk with Christ, it is important to keep the MAIN THING, the MAIN THING." In other words, don't get sidetracked by all types of new "isms," new interpretations of the Word, new revelations, new personality cults, all that can take us away from the faith grounded and steadfast in the hope of the gospel. My hope is still built on nothing less than Jesus.

Today, revisit the first teachers, preacher, parents, and friends that helped give you the basics of the gospel. In your mind, thank God for each of them that helped with your foundation. I go back to Sunday school teachers that put up with hyper children and belligerent teenagers, each week sharing the message against great odds. I remember the night of a Billy Graham rally going forward in Greensboro, North Carolina, and making my decision for Christ. But then I remember a dear friend, George Douglas, clinching the nail that Billy Graham drove in. Each of those mentioned, I pray for today. They helped a rebellious sinner find the faith and now continue in it these many years later.

"I'm possessed for a hope that is steadfast and sure since Jesus came into my heart." *–Gospel song*

~ 103 ~

Colossians 1:27 (NIV) – *"Which is Christ in you, the hope of glory."*

Notice the words IN YOU. Christ in you. What a challenging

thought. God uses me to bring hope. Roger Palms, in his book Bible Readings on Hope uses an interesting phrase—Hope BRINGER. You and I are in the ministry of bringing hope. Wow! Get blessed with that thought today. "I am a hope bringer."

The letter of Colossians was written from prison. Paul was imprisoned in the city of Rome where he wrote four letters often referred to as the prison epistles. Our prisons today are a far cry from ancient places of incarceration. Having been a part of prison ministries for many years, I have seen an evolution of the facilities where prisoners are now housed. In addition, they are provided libraries, fitness centers, computers, TVs, and other amenities that had nothing in common with the incarceration of Paul. This was revealed to me dramatically on a tour of Rome a number of years ago. Our guide took us into a drab-looking room, pointed to a hole in the floor, and had each of us get on our knees and look down into the cell beneath the floor. Tradition has it that Paul was confined to such a cell, and it was there he wrote this letter containing a message on hope. Paul was a "hope bringer," even while waiting his execution in Rome.

Max Lucado, in his book entitled *Grace*, gives an amazing story of someone giving hope. Tara Storch lost her daughter in a terrible skiing accident. The daughter, Taylor, was just thirteen. Following the horrific event and the personal struggles that evolved, they decided to donate their daughter's organs to needy patients. Her heart was given to Patricia Winters. Taylor's heart gave new life to Patricia, who had suffered for years. Weeks later, Tara and her husband flew to Dallas to hear their daughter's heart beating within the recipient. That's right—each mother placed the stethoscope to their ear and listened. Can you

Dave Bailey

imagine your daughter's heart beating within another person, bringing hope to them of new life? Taylor, even after her death, was a hope bringer to a girl she didn't even know.

Someone wrote, "We are a missionary or a mission field. If we know Christ, we are missionaries; if we don't know Christ, we are a mission field." Think of this in terms of today's Scripture. If we know Christ, we have a mission to bring hope to those who don't know Christ. All of us are placed in some mission field. I am in the mission field of bringing hope to troubled youth, but each of us are surrounded by those who need "hope bringers"—families struggling with the death of a loved one, or people going through emotional difficulties, job loss, church division, etc. The needs are endless. Christ is in you today, so give out the message. We expect to succeed.

> "There is no medicine like hope, no incentive so great, and no tonic so powerful as expectation of something better tomorrow." *–Orison Swett Marden*

~ 104 ~

1 Thessalonians 1:3 (NKJV) – *"Remembering without ceasing your work of faith, labor of love, and patience of hope in our Lord Jesus Christ."*

This letter to Thessalonica was one of the first written by Paul. It was probably written from Corinth about 51 AD. This is less than twenty years after the death and resurrection of Jesus. Paul and Silas went to this European city after Paul had a vision of a man from Macedonia. The man urged him to come and preach the gospel. And Paul responded by writing this letter; it is a very encouraging one. Paul commends them on their good example—work of faith, labor of love, and patience of hope. What makes it so remarkable is that this was not an easy place to live for Christ. Historians say it was very hostile to the gospel! Think you're in a tough environment, read on.

Thessalonica was a seaport. Traditionally seaports were places of immorality—men with money and time off looking for a good time. It was one of the wealthiest trade centers of the Roman Empire. Not a very fertile mission field, and yet as the Scriptures say, "Where sin did abound, grace did much more abound." So Paul tells the young church he remembers their patience of hope. In a city of great wealth and a diverse and changing population, Paul focused on their patience in reaching others with the gospel. We, too, need that kind of patience.

All of us have practiced some work of faith and labor of love. Sometimes there have been positive results, and other times we have been left exhausted with little fruit from our efforts. That's when patience of hope must kick in.

I remember hearing a Korean pastor, Rev. Paul Choo, speak in Washington, DC. He told of starting a church in Seoul at an old laundromat. The first Sunday service, twenty people attended. Undaunted, he told us of praying like a mother hen over an empty nest. Clucking like a chicken, he sat on twenty-five eggs (each egg was to represent a new member for the church). The first month one hundred eggs, the next month, and on and on. They moved from the laundromat when five hundred eggs had hatched. Today the church has over twenty-five thousand members. But it started with the word of faith, labor of love, and patience of hope.

Patience of hope can do that for you. Start by building your nest of eggs (whatever the eggs will represent). Faithfully pray that God will give you the increase as each egg hatches. Spend time on your nest even if it is in the most hostile environment.

"When the world says give up, hope whispers try it one more time." –*Cindy Hess Kasper*

~ 105 ~

1 Thessalonians 2:19 (NKJV) – *"For what is our hope, or joy, or crown of rejoicing? Is it not even you in the presence of our Lord Jesus Christ at His coming?"*

Have you ever tried to see someone and you were hindered at every attempt? This has often happened when I have wanted to see a friend that was very ill. More often than not, I have arrived too late and they passed away.

Paul, in today's study, has been trying to visit the believers at Thessalonica. For a number of reasons (including Satan and persecution), it has been impossible. This city was very hostile to the church, and Paul had to make a quick departure, leaving a young, immature group of believers. But he was concerned for its survival. Paul traveled to Athens and sent Timothy to Thessalonica to encourage believers and bring a word of hope.

A motion picture was released to a limited number of theaters called *For Greater Glory*. Unfortunately, as with many faith-based films, it also was seen by a limited number of people. My wife and I went to its initial showing. We were overwhelmed with the story and its relevance to today, even though it was based on events in Mexico during the 1930s.

The story took place during the presidency of Plutarco Elías Calles, serving from 1924–1928. He also continued to hold sway on politics for the next twelve years. Calles was against the Mexican Catholic Church. He persecuted the church, killed followers of Christ, destroyed churches, and exported church leaders and priests who were not Mexican. Christians initially were passive in meeting this opposition, but then peasants organized to fight back. They were derisively called *Christeros* or Christers. Their battle cry was *Viva Cristo Rey!* (Long live Christ the king.)

You must see the film to appreciate the numerous plots and subplots, but one theme is so relevant. Every generation of Christians must challenge any government that takes away religious freedom. Often it is more subtle than the experience in Mexico. Laws are passed that erode the church's right to dissent when the government tempts to dictate morality from a secular viewpoint.

The word from Paul was important then and today. In spite of all the opposition and persecution the young church faced, Paul wanted them to look past that and find hope and joy in the presence of Christ. Every generation of Christians has faced some form of hostility. Sometimes it is quite obvious and other times very subtle. Jesus gave us a great teaching for such times. "In this world you will have tribulation, but I have overcome the world." Today be an overcomer, and receive your hope, joy, and crown of rejoicing. The Christians of Mexico were ultimately successful and survived the attempt to destroy them.

"His Word my hope secures." *—John Newton "Amazing Grace"*

~ 106 ~

1 Thessalonians 4:13 (NIV) – *"Brothers and sisters, we do not want you to be uninformed about those who sleep in death, so that you do not grieve like the rest of mankind, who have no hope."*

We have all attended funerals—sometimes for family, friends, or other associates. Today they are called memorial services, celebrations of life, or some other euphemism. Obviously, in my fifty-five years of ministry I have officiated at a wide variety of funerals. Some services are conducted for people I never met, and I minister mainly for the family. It is difficult to eulogize a person about whom you know very little, but the main message is always the same. For the believers there is hope in the face of death. I must admit that it is a joy, a blessed experience when I lead a celebration of life for one who has known and served the Lord.

Paul, writing to the Christians of Thessalonica, uses the phrase "those who fall asleep." Some have taken this to mean we literally fall asleep and remain unconscious until the Lord returns. Others believe this is just a nice way to describe death, like we say today "passed away" or "went home to be with the Lord." However, we interpret this that the good news is we have hope (expectation of success) that at death we will go to be with Him. As the old spiritual says, "Ain't no grave gonna hold this body down!"

When I was a little boy, family friends had a farm in Delaware. They had me visit with them a couple of days, and I enjoyed working (?) and playing in the barn and the open fields of the one-hundred-acre farm (even got to drive a John Deere tractor). On the night I was to go home, my Dad was to come down in

boys thrown into battle at such a young age and often losing their lives. Lopez could have been just another statistic in the horror of warfare, but this was not to be the case. By the grace of God he escaped from his imprisonment during the night, ran three days, and ended up in a refugee camp in Kenya. During his time in the camp, he was given the opportunity to come to America. Through a miraculous series of events he became a citizen of America, graduated from college, and excelled in athletics. Not only did he excel, but he became a member of the American Olympic team. He never owned a pair of shoes, but now Nike is his official sponsor. It is a story that should be told to all who want to wear the helmet of hope. Lopez's message inspires us today to sober up, or stay sober during the days of evil.

"All kids need is a little help, a little hope, and someone who believes in them." *–Magic Johnson*

~ 108 ~

2 Thessalonians 2:16–17 (NKJV) – *"Now may our Lord Jesus Christ Himself, and our God and Father, who has loved us and given us everlasting consolation and good hope by grace, comfort your hearts and establish you in every good word and work."*

A gift from God —good hope. These two verses from 2 Thessalonians read almost like a benediction or a blessing at the close of a service of worship. But actually they are a prelude to a service of instruction, concluding with how to disciple a church member. Ever notice that disciple and discipline come from the same root word for "teach"? So after Paul encourages believers, he then must discuss the difficult task of dealing with evil in the church, so he writes, "Admonish him as brethren; don't keep company with him."

However, our focus is on "good hope." How are we to have good hope? Well, Paul makes it clear that God has given us good hope by grace. We don't deserve it, we can't work for it; it is His gift to the believer. Like any gift from God, it is the result of His character and we don't merit it. That has always been difficult to understand, especially in a culture where gifts are usually the result of something we do. That's what makes God's grace amazing.

This became clear to me recently in an experience Susan Piper shared. Susan is a gospel singer and songwriter who ministers in nursing homes. She told of a lady in a nursing home who said she loved the hymn "Amazing Grace" except for the phrase (can you guess which one?) "that saved a wretch like me." She didn't feel like a wretch. But the hymn writer, John Newton, did. A former slave trader, he knew God's grace saved him from a life outside Christ, a life that led him to do deplorable things to fellow human beings. The only difference between that woman and John Newton was the degree and type of sin. She missed an important foundation block in the gospel—"All have sinned and fallen short." (We are all wretched.) Therefore, we all need God's grace. Susan Piper was fully aware of the "good hope by grace," as she came from a dysfunctional family and lifestyle. Like Susan, our hope is built on God's amazing grace.

> "There's quite enough hope and quite enough power to chase away any gloom, for Jesus, Lord Jesus is in this very room." *–Ron and Carol H.*

~ **109** ~

1 Timothy 1:1 (NKJV) – *"Paul, an apostle of Jesus Christ, by the commandment of God our Savior and the Lord Jesus Christ, our hope."*

Did anyone ever question your credentials? For instance, has someone requested proof that you have a driver's license (usually a state trooper if you are stopped for speeding)? Maybe a card to prove you are on Medicare or have a hospitalization policy? Interestingly enough for me, I had a pastor in another denomination question my credentials as an ordained, seminary graduate. He belonged to a church that traced its history back to St. Peter. It was my pleasure to trace the history of my denomination also back to St. Peter. Needless to say, it was fun to go over our family tree and show how all the branches (including his) went back to a common root. We were going to assist each other in an interfaith marriage; you can imagine it turned into quite a discussion. Our study today begins with Paul establishing his credentials in a similar fashion as he writes to Timothy.

The letter starts with these words, "Paul, an apostle of Jesus Christ." That says it all about Paul's credibility. He is an apostle, a sent one. There is no doubt about it—Paul declares he is an AMBASSADOR on a mission sent by Jesus the Christ. Of course, there were those who questioned his credentials, but his authority came from two main sources: God our Savior and the Lord Jesus Christ. Having reviewed this important issue, Paul can then move on to focusing on the Lord Jesus Christ as the foundation of our hope.

Remember every word has special meaning for Paul. As he writes a letter, he must think of how the reader will interpret his message. It is one thing to speak to people directly and respond to questions; it is another to communicate by the written word. Thus there is a reason he uses hope in this context. First he had expectations of success in this present world. Hope was for the now! Timothy, as a young preacher, needed to know that, and so do we. Paul was teaching Christianity 101—a basic fact. Hope was important as Timothy took over the church of Ephesus. Every young preacher starting with a young church needs to bring hope to his people, and we better know that hope is real for us living today.

But Paul also wanted Timothy to know hope was for the future. It is because of Jesus that with great expectation we can look forward to heaven. That was good news for those new Christians, the first generation to hear the gospel. And stop to think it has been passed on from generation to generation, nation to nation, culture to culture, and now we have that hope of glory. I often think of the generations of my family before me that were encouraged by the preaching of the gospel. Now it is my turn.

"When you feel like giving up, remember why hope helped you hang on in the first place." *—Anonymous*

~ 110 ~

1 Timothy 4:9–10 (NIV) – *"This is a trustworthy saying that deserves full acceptance. That is why we labor and strive, because we have put our hope in the living God."*

It was communion Sunday. Since a child in youth choir, I had heard the familiar ritual leading up to taking the bread and cup. (We take grape juice in our tradition—no wine.) Like any ritual or liturgy, it can become routine, and the repetition can take away its deep meaning. Until I was writing today's study I had no idea that one particular part of the service was taken directly from the letter to Timothy. In our communion service we recite the words: "This is a trustworthy saying and worthy of all acceptation that Christ Jesus died for our sins." Every time we take communion we are reaffirming the hope that Christ died for our sins. Is it any wonder Christ told us to do this in remembrance of Him?

Leaving these thoughts about communion, we now turn to these words that are written to Timothy as a minister of the gospel. Paul tells him to be a good minister. Notice the words preceding today's verse: "Teach the truth, not old fables, train yourself to be godly, emphasize spiritual exercise more than physical workouts, concentrate on the eternal, not just today." Of course, this is important for a minister, but it applies to all of us who want to put our hope in the living God.

One of the great teachings of the Protestant Reformation was the "priesthood of all believers." Martin Luther, with this teaching, did not want to deprecate the priest and his role in the church but rather elevate the laity. In the church during Luther's time, some of the clergy and hierarchy had used and abused power. The average person felt disenfranchised and insignificant in the grand scheme of the kingdom.

Luther and other reformers wanted to have all believers see their responsibilities as "ministers of the gospel." I sometimes feel that today we need another reformation of hope. Hope in the living God throughout the church that takes all of us into ministry.

One final thought. Years ago when I first was called to start Ranch Hope, a minister friend said he was saddened that I was leaving the ministry. I was shocked. What he meant was I was leaving the local church pastoral ministry, but he did not say that. His implication was that I would no longer be a preacher, but a social worker and administrator. He missed the importance of the ministry of all believers. For over fifty years I have ministered to troubled youth. Where has the Lord called you to bring hope?

> "Three great essentials to happiness in this life revolve around something to do, something to be, and something to hope for." –*Joseph Addison*

~ 111 ~

Titus 1:2 (KJV) – *"Hope of eternal life."*

"Paul, a slave of God and an apostle of Jesus Christ." What a way to open a letter to Titus as he ministers on the island of Create. He describes himself as a slave and an apostle. Previously we covered the word apostle (sent one); now we focus for a moment on "slave of God." The word from Greek means a bondsman, one who is subject to the will of his master. Titus, and the members of the church on Crete, would understand the word and the implications for a believer. A bondservant to God, Paul was describing himself as one in complete submission to God. Is this a description of you and me?

In ancient Rome the Empire depended on slavery. Each slave owner had his own brand that was placed on a slave, like we would brand cattle today. We have a rodeo close to the Ranch called Cowtown. The owner, Grant Harris, brands all of his livestock with a CT. It shows ownership of each horse and steer. In Paul's day, wherever that slave traveled, he was clearly marked (often on the forehead) by his owner's brand. Paul states in one letter, "I bear in my body, the brand of the Lord Jesus." Paul knew that brands could also denote religious and military allegiance. Alexander the Great had his soldiers branded with A— Alpha. Wherever they went, people knew they were committed to Alexander. Paul would say, as we should, "I bear in my body the brand of Christ." We too are a bondservant of God. Bondservants have responsibilities. So the theme of this letter is defining how Christians act in a life of submission.

Paul is instructing Titus to teach the Cretans the importance of working out their salvation. Good works are important, and good leadership was needed in this island church off the coast of Greece. Crete was a wealthy little place, but with it came all the excesses of prosperity. So Paul wanted Titus to carefully teach what represented a godly life so believers could have the hope of eternal life. The old adage still makes sense: "Heaven is a prepared place for prepared people." Those of us enslaved to God are assured of that prepared place.

Do you today have hope for eternal life? Do we bear in our bodies the brand (not the tattoo) of the Lord Jesus? Of course, that is our greatest expectation of success. Our final chapter is not the end of our story; it is the beginning of a new chapter, and wow, what a new beginning!

"What the caterpillar calls the end of the world, the master calls a butterfly." *–Richard Bach*

~ 112 ~

Titus 2:13 (NIV) – *"While we wait for the blessed hope—the appearing of the glory of our great God and Savior, Jesus Christ."*

Waiting is not one of my virtues. Whether it is in the doctor's office, at an airport, or for my grandchild to arrive. Can you relate? Over the years, however, I have had to grow in the area of patience; hope helps us in this arena of life. Hope helps us wait and gives us a reason to wait. This is particularly true in today's study—waiting for the return of our Lord Jesus.

Since the early church, Christians have been "looking for the blessed hope." Titus, as a young preacher on the island of Crete, had a church that was argumentative, split over dogma, and in need of strong leadership. Paul had traveled to Titus, was a good friend of the young preacher, and thus gave important assistance in dealing with a troubled church. Parts of that instruction were helping the Cretans look beyond their own society and culture and see a new life in Christ. For those island people and for us today, we live a godly life, and that prepares us for the blessed hope of our Lord's return.

In every church there are some who obsess over the return of our Lord. Constantly looking for "signs," they lose focus and concentrate on the signs instead of the hope. While traveling through Arizona a few years ago, my family and I noticed that an upcoming town would have a sign every mile telling us something about the town and distance still to travel to reach it. I thought to myself, "Suppose we become obsessed by these signs, stopped to study each one, lingered and lingered in the middle of the deserted wilderness—we would have never reached our destination." Signs are just signs. They point us to our goal. Titus, in his letter, underlines this spiritual truth. Keep looking for our Lord's return; it is a blessed hope.

But, of course, the return of our Lord is also a warning. A flashing sign—caution. Stop. Look. Listen! Danger! Jesus told us He would return as a thief in the night, so be ready. Remember the wise and foolish virgins; keep our lights lighted, because the bridegroom comes when he is least expected. So it is with the Lord Jesus. You might remember a song written during the Jesus Movement era, lamenting, "Life was filled with guns and war and everyone got trampled on the floor; a man and wife asleep in bed, she turns her head and he is gone, and she was left behind. I wish we'd all been ready!" This song of the sixties called upon that generation to get ready for the return of our Lord. Many thought the signs were everywhere for the second coming of Jesus. But once again we learned every generation must be ready. Today we can be ready for His return, living a godly life and looking for the blessed hope.

"Hope never abandons us; we abandon hope." *–George Weinberg*

208

~ **113** ~

Titus 3:7 (NIV) – *"Having been justified by his grace, we might become heirs having the hope of eternal life."*

Heirs of God; joined heirs with Jesus! All that God has belongs to us. What an inheritance! Titus gives the Christians of Crete an important teaching; it is a part of our education today. If we are justified by His grace, we now have hope for eternal life. Modern translation: When we accept Christ as Savior, it is just as if we had never sinned, and His love makes us a part of the family of God forever. At the reading of the will we get blessed; hope is one of God's eternal gifts.

When my nephew Jimmy died a few years ago, my niece (his sister) Beverly sent me this e-mail. It tells his story of hope— found late in life, but still found. I have printed the e-mail in its entirety. It is a message of hope for family members still seeking the truth.

MY BROTHER DIED TODAY
HE WAS 60 YEARS AND 9 DAYS OLD—
LAST WEEK HE WAS DIAGNOSED WITH LUNG CANCER.
IT HAD SPREAD.
HE HAD SMOKED SINCE HE WAS 12 YEARS OLD
YESTERDAY THEY CALLED HOSPICE
I HAVE SEEN HIM TWICE IN 35 YEARS
HE WAS 3 WHEN I WENT TO LIVE WITH MY GRANDPARENTS
SO OUR "EXPOSURE" TO EACH OTHER WAS CONFINED TO A FEW WEEKS OF THE YEAR

HE CHOSE A "DIFFERENT" LIFE STYLE AS HE GREW—

ALCOHOL— DRUGS—- AND A VIOLENT TEMPER DESTROYING CHANCES AS A LEFT HAND PITCHER IN BASEBALL—-

HE PREFERRED BARROOM BRAWLS WITH ARRESTS TO SPRINGTRAINING—

HE CHOSE AWOL AND DISOBEYING ORDERS IN THE MARINE CORPS —-

THE OPPORTUNITY TO SERVE AT AN EMBASSY ATTACHED TO AN AMBASSADOR –DESTROYED WHEN HE CHOSE THE FORMER METHODS—-

HIS TEMPER DESTROYED ALMOST EVERYTHING HE TOUCHED—

I SAY ALMOST —

BECAUSE 17 YEARS AGO MY BROTHER MET JANICE WHO WOULD BECOME HIS THIRD WIFE—

SHE WAS VERY LOVING DURING THE TUMULTUOUS FIRST 5 YEARS —

JANICE IS A CHRISTIAN—

10 YEARS AGO MY BROTHER GAVE HIS LIFE TO THE LIVING CHRIST AND OPENED HIS HEART TO JESUS—

HE WAS BAPTIZED / JOINED THE CHURCH THEY ATTENDED—

HE SANG SOLOS / HE GAVE WITNESS / TAUGHT SUNDAY SCHOOL

HE SANG AT OUR MOTHER'S MEMORIAL SERVICE 3 YEARS AGO

SO WHEN THE DOCTOR SAID GET YOUR LIFE IN ORDER —

HIS LIFE WAS IN ORDER
MY BROTHER DIED TODAY
And went HOME.

Don't give up hope on your loved one or friend; there is still time for them to receive their inheritance.

"Hope is like the sun, which, as you journey toward it, casts the shadow of our burden behind us." *–Samuel Smiles*

~ 114 ~

Hebrews 3:6 (NKJV) – *"Christ as a Son over His own house, whose house we are if we hold fast the confidence and the rejoicing of the hope."*

The author of the letter to the Hebrews puts the word hope in an unusual context. Therefore, before we find our inspirational thought from this verse, we must know what precedes it. The author makes comparisons between Moses and Jesus. Because this is a letter written to Jewish Christians, it is the writer's attempt to answer questions raised about Jesus and Moses. Jewish comics often joke, "Jesus saves, but Moses invests." The letter to the Hebrews shows the serious differences between these two great Jewish leaders. It hinges on Moses being the lawgiver and Jesus the Messiah.

Simply speaking, this letter underlines that Moses' work pointed toward the Messiah. Moses' law made it clear that man is sinful and in need of salvation, and Jesus provided that salvation as

211

Messiah. To illustrate further, the analogy of a house is used. This analogy points us to hope. Moses was faithful in the house of God, but Jesus ruled over the house. It is the difference between renting a house (Moses) and owning the house (Jesus). The house, for the writer, was also symbolic of the church. So, for Jesus, the Messiah, the house contained all those who believed in Him.

Now we can review the message of hope today. The message is clear for the new Jewish Christians: hold fast the confidence and the rejoicing of hope you now have in Jesus. Three phrases stand out: hold fast, confidence, and rejoicing in hope. They are as important today as they were for those who read the letter of Hebrews for the first time. Hope will help us endure confidently (with faith) to the end, to the end of our lives, or to the end of time.

I can't leave this study without calling attention to rejoicing in hope. Hope does bring joy. There is still joy in knowing Jesus. The early Jewish Christians needed that instruction, and so do we. Years ago in my first pastorate, I passed two Sunday school classes—one a children's group, the other a group of seniors. The children were involved in a booming rendition of "I've got the joy, joy, joy , joy down in my heart," and the seniors were somberly studying. I prayed that some of that joy would invade the seniors. The older we get, the more we need "rejoicing of hope."

> "No matter what life does to us, God offers us restoration and hope." –*Dan Nelson*

~ 115 ~

Hebrews 6:9 – *"Your best days are ahead."* 6:11 –
"Make your hope seen until the end—don't be sluggish."

Your best days are ahead—really? Can the author of Hebrews be serious? At what point in our life can we say that with assurance? Maybe in our youth we could say this, facing the future with anticipation. Possibly as we begin a career or marriage or new business or whatever, but as life progresses and age settles in, can we still believe the BEST days are ahead? Only if we progress to Verse 11: "Make your hope seen to the end." Our expectations of success will be with us right to the very end.

The funeral was a difficult one. The couple had been married nearly sixty-five years, but now the wife had died. Her husband stood near the casket; the last of the friends and family had spoken to him and offered their condolences. His pastor stood close by after conducting the memorial service and tried to console him. "When Margaret and I were dating, we looked forward to marriage, and a door opened and we were married. We wanted children, and a few years later the door to being parents opened. Time passed, and we looked forward to retirement and grandchildren. The door opened, we retired, and enjoyed our grandchildren. Now she's gone; no more doors," his voice trailed off as he sobbed uncontrollably.

His pastor stepped closer and, placing his arm around his aged friend, said, "Remember there is one more door." Jesus said, "I am the door. Your wife has entered through one more door." It took awhile for healing to begin, but the husband was given hope by the words of his pastor. Every door is an entrance and an exit. We enter a door for the kitchen; we exit the same door for the garden.

There is a famous painting of a door in a garden setting. Jesus stands knocking at the door; usually He is holding a lantern. If you look closely, you will notice there is no latch on the outside. Jesus cannot open the door from the outside. We must open it from the inside, and then He can enter. There was a time when this man's wife had opened the door to Christ, and now she had entered into eternal life. This story has often blessed me.

> If I knew it would be the last time that I'd see you fall asleep, I would tuck you in more tightly and pray the Lord, your soul to keep.

> If I knew it would be the last time that I see you walk out the door, I would give you a hug and kiss and call you back for one more.

> If I knew it would be the last time I'd hear your voice lifted up in praise, I would videotape each action and word, so I could play them back day after day.

> If I knew it would be the last time, I would spare an extra minute or two to stop and say, "I love you," instead of assuming, you would know I do.

> If I knew it would be the last time I would be there to share your day, Well, I'm sure you'll have so many more, so I can let just this one slip away.

> For surely there's always tomorrow to make up for an

oversight, and we always get a second chance to make everything right.

There will always be another day to say, "I love you," and certainly there's another chance to say our "Anything I can do's?"

But just in case I might be wrong and today is all I get, I'd like to say how much I love you, and I hope we never forget, tomorrow is not promised to anyone, young or old alike. And today may be the last chance you get to hold your loved one tight.

So if you're waiting for tomorrow, why not do it today? For if tomorrow never comes, you'll surely regret the day that you didn't take that extra time for a smile, a hug, or a kiss, and you were too busy to grant someone what turned out to be their one last wish.

So hold your loved ones close today, whisper in their ear, tell them how much you love them and that you'll always hold them dear. Take time to say, "I'm sorry," "please forgive me," "thank you," or "it's okay."

And if tomorrow never comes, you'll have no regrets.

Our best days are ahead—if our life is built upon hope. The body and mind go through changes. Our circle of friends and activities grow less and less, but we will not be sluggish; we will expect to succeed to the end.

"We have always held to the hope, the belief, the conviction that there is a better life, a better world, beyond the horizon." *–Franklin D. Roosevelt*

~ 116 ~

Hebrews 6:18 (NIV*)* – *"Take hold of the hope set before us [Get a grip]."*

The book (letter) of Hebrews was written especially for Christians with a Jewish heritage who had started doubting their faith and conversion experience. It is actually written more like a sermon than a book or letter. The author wants to bring hope to Jews who are struggling with their newfound faith in Jesus as Messiah. Now these many centuries later, the words can inspire our generation of Christians to "take hold of the hope that is set before you."

Often we have read that God does not let go of us; we are in the palm of His hands, but this verse reminds us that we must not lose our hold on God, and that comes by way of hope. A modern translation could be: God does not lie, so get a grip. Get a grip and don't let go! We teach our children to hold our hand when crossing the street or walking in a mall. It is our way of protecting them from some unexpected event. Children often react by pulling back and saying, "I can do it myself." After an unexpected fall, misstep, or worse an accident, they realize the value of holding on to Mom and Dad.

Author and preacher Chuck Swindoll, in one of his books, tells of an experience with his family. After church one Sunday, he, his wife, and his young children drove up into the California mountains for lunch. After their picnic, they descended a winding road when a sudden snow shower blanketed the road and obscured their vision. Inadvertently, Chuck hit the brakes, and the car skidded out of control. His wife and children screamed, and he panicked. By the grace of God, the spinning car hit a stretch of dry pavement, and the tires gripped the road, causing the car to stop. The grip of the tires on the dry pavement prevented a catastrophe. Not only is that an important reminder to have good tires—bald ones will not do—but it is a spiritual message.

Chuck Swindoll uses the illustration to refresh our memory about the importance of keeping a good grip on God. Our emphasis for today's devotion would be, "Hope helps us keep our grip." Throughout today, remember we have the same promise given to Abraham; we are heirs of the promise. God hasn't changed. Keep holding on!

> "Hope founded in Christ enables us to squarely face the dark days." –*Alistair Begg*

~ 117 ~

Hebrews 6:19 (NIV) – *"We have this hope as an anchor for the soul, firm and secure."*

The author of Hebrews gave us the word hope in the form of our grip. We think of hope as an anchor to the soul. Notice the author of Hebrews adds two words after the comma—firm and secure. This is not an anchor that is being dragged through the sand; it is gripped to something that holds.

Years ago, as a young preacher, I would lead hymn singing after our Sunday night service. (That's right—Sunday night services.) Once a month, churches from the area in Southern New Jersey would come together in a host church for one hour of singing hymns. An award (a banner) was given each month to the church bringing the most participants. It was very competitive and greatly inspirational. People of all age groups joined organ, piano, and a small traveling bad to sing great old hymns of the church.

It became a tradition that the hymn singing would build toward a great climax. Everyone took for granted that the participants would save their best voices and energy for "My Anchor Holds," a moving gospel song that took each of us from "though the angry surge roll o'er my tempest driven soul" to "I've an anchor that will even more endure." We were expressing in music those Sunday nights what the meditation from Hebrews today expresses in the written word—God does not change. He is our anchor. He is firm and secure. Whatever storm, whatever challenges, whatever we confront in our walk with the Lord, hope (expectation of success) is our anchor.

In her book *Hope for the Heart*, noted speaker, writer, and radio host June Hunt writes, "Christian Hope is –

> Not dependent on other people or a group of people, but rather dependent on the Lord alone."

> Not wishful thinking, but is unchangeable and absolute.

> Not determined by circumstances or events, but on what is secure and absolute.

Not relying on stars, luck, chance, or timing, but by what is settled in the heart and mind of God.

"Hope for the Christian is a certainty . . . because its basis is Christ." *–David McCasland*

~ 118 ~

Hebrews 7:19 (NIV) – *"And a better hope is introduced, by which we draw near to God."*

A better hope. Better than what? Hebrews tells us that Christians have a better hope with Jesus the Messiah. A better hope for the Jews drawing near to God. This, of course, was a turnoff to many Jews; it was heresy. But for the believer, it was the expectation of success.

It might be beneficial to read the entire seventh chapter. Remember, it is written to the Hebrews, especially those Jews who knew Jesus—from legalism to grace, attempting to help them in their transition. Many could not accept such a transition. The author goes all the way back to Melchizedek, king of Salem, a priest and king. He is a prefigure of Jesus, like the son of God, but not the same. Neither he nor the Levitical priesthood could save; that's why the Messiah Jesus came for Jews and Gentiles. It is Jesus that puts the better in hope.

Now focus on the words "by which we draw near to God." Review with me the words of the beloved hymn: "Nearer, my God, to thee, nearer to thee! Even though it be the cross that raiseth me; still all my song shall be, nearer, my God, to thee; nearer, my God, to thee; nearer to thee."

Sarah Adams wrote these words in the nineteenth century after she had lived through some difficult times. Her mother died when she was five, and at the age of thirty-two she had to retire from the theater because of failing health. Add to this disappointment her sister's health failing and Sarah's fear that her sister would die. Her pastor challenged Sarah to write a hymn to go along with his message on Jacob's ladder. The result was the hymn "Nearer, My God, to Thee." Sarah Adams, in her own life, learned that negative experiences can draw us nearer to God.

Today remember these great truths:

> The Lord is near to all who call upon Him (Psalm 145:18).
> [He hasn't moved.] He is near, count on it.
> He will not forsake us (Psalm 9:10).
> We can trust God.
> If with our heart you truly seek
> Me, you will find me!
> God doesn't play hide and go seek.
> And finally the words of Jesus. Matthew 7:7:
> "Ask and it will be given you, seek and you will find, knock and it will be opened to you."

As we remember these truths, it will give us a better hope. (Maybe we will be introduced to it for the first time, and it will help us draw near to God.)

> "When you say a situation or person is hopeless, you are slamming the door in the face of God." *–Charles L. Allen*

220

~ **119** ~

Hebrews 10:23 (NKJV) – *"Let us hold fast the confession of our hope without wavering, for He who promised is faithful."*

He was a visitor to the local mall. It was one of those crowded days (probably sales galore). But as a reluctant shopper assisting his wife find bargains, he was not prepared for the message emblazed on a woman's T-shirt. Big, bold letters proclaimed her negative message: "HOPE IS FOR SUCKERS." He thought to himself, "What in the world happened in this woman's life that caused her to reach that conclusion?" Can you imagine sitting down with her and listening to her litany of complaints? Was it a love relationship that went south, health issues, the loss of a job, rebellious children, etc.?

As I read this story I thought to myself, this woman needs a copy of this book. A person who thinks hope is for suckers needs to know the message of the Word, like Hebrews 10:23. "Let us hold fast . . . [to] hope [expectation of success] without wavering, for He who promised is faithful."

I want to contrast that T-shirt with a message we had printed on the back of our jackets at Ranch Hope. Read it with me. Ranch Hope: "My hope is built on nothing less than Jesus." The writer of Hebrews would be much more content with our jacket than the lady's T-shirt. This author was writing from the perspective of assurance, not wishful thinking. His hope was in God, and he challenged those who read his epistle to hold on fast, without wavering, to the ONE who is faithful. This phrase "hold on" is mentioned a number of times in Hebrews, so we know the writer believes it is important. Don't let go!

Is it possible there was a time when the lady with the T-shirt was a believer? Is it possible there was a time when she had hope and then the bottom fell out? I have read the book Killing Kennedy by Bill O'Reilly and Martin Dugard. In one chapter they talk about the fictitious Camelot. There were those who characterized the presidency of John F. Kennedy as Camelot, but then the tragedy of assassination happened. I wondered if Jackie Kennedy lost all hope. I wondered if there was anyone in her life that pointed her to the hope that sees beyond Camelot. Every one of us have had tragedies that test us and cause us to doubt and speculate, what if? Again—don't let go! Or let go—let God!

One final thought. Jackie Kennedy, in an interview with *Life* magazine, revealed the story that JFK often listened to the soundtrack of the musical *Camelot*. He especially liked the final line, "Don't let it be forgot, that once there was a spot, for one brief shining moment, that was known as Camelot." There are no Camelots on this earth. If we believe in them, they bring disappointment—hope is for suckers. It is a grand musical and love story, but our love story is about a Savior. A Savior who was the lover of our soul and died that we might have the ultimate Camelot—eternity with God.

"No night is so dark nor day so cloudy that can cancel the hope that this too shall pass." *–Michael Guido*

~ 120 ~

1 Peter 1:3 (NIV) – *"He has given us new birth into a living hope through the resurrection of Jesus Christ from the dead."*

The vocalist was singing a "goldy oldie" gospel song, but its message was relevant to all of us listening. "Born again, there's really been a change in me, born again just like Jesus said."

Peter writes, "He has given us new birth." Yes, we have been born again. Now how that rebirth takes place has been interpreted various ways in various churches. For some, it has taken place at baptism, for some at confirmation, for some a gradual process, for others an instant radical transformation. The important thing is not HOW, but if, and do we have the assurance it happened to us?

Our study today tells us we can trust because of that new birth. We now have a living hope through the resurrection of Jesus Christ from the dead. Reflect on that for a moment. New birth—new hope—new life—no death. It all makes sense. It all matters. It is not a dead end street. It is not all an accident of the universe. You are not an accident of blind chance. You can live a life with expectation of success in the here and the hereafter.

I grew up with two older sisters and three older brothers. Being the last one, I often took the brunt of jokes about being the "baby" and also had to face the possibility I was an accident. My closest brother would often repeat, "David, you weren't supposed to be here; you're an accident." Of course, being the "baby," I was also greatly spoiled, but the accident thing often made me think—was I unplanned? Realistically, I imagine most of you reading this book are "accidents," biologically speaking, but there are no accidents in the plan of God.

Think today of how blessed we are because of Jesus. We have the "best of both worlds." Born again into new life on earth and with hope to live eternally with God. Wow! It is a living hope.

Today reaffirm your rebirth; reaffirm your hope because of the resurrection. Reaffirm that you are not an accident. And live life according to His plan.

> Prayer: "God of compassion, send your Spirit to strengthen those who have no strength, to bring peace to those who have no peace, and give hope to all in despair. Amen." *–Carol Griffin*

~ 121 ~

1 Peter 1:13 (NKJV) – *"Rest your hope fully upon the grace that is to be brought to you at the revelation of Jesus Christ."*

The world has never been a friend of grace. (And I'm not talking about "a blue-eyed blonde," as one author wrote.) Since the gospel was first proclaimed, critics, detractors, and persecutors have done their best to eradicate the faith once and forever delivered to the saints. Peter writes his first letter to the church in Asia Minor where they are suffering persecution. His theme—rest your hope solely on the grace of God brought to you at the revelation of Jesus Christ. Whatever distractions we may face today, that is a good word from Peter for us.

This verse is preceded by some additional good advice. "Gird up the loins of your mind." Say what? Well, the message was evident for those who first read this letter. People in that time would pull up their long robes—fasten them around their waist so they could move quickly with no hindrance from the material. I remember doing this as a small boy when wearing a choir robe. Goofing off with the other guys, we would chase each other back to Sunday school. It helped to pull up the robe to run faster. Peter is writing that we must do whatever it takes to focus on seeing God. Pull up whatever encumbers our service. Stay focused!

Peter also writes, "Be sober." Sober in this context has special meaning for us. He admonishes us to think clearly, mentally and spiritually, so we can make good decisions. It is of little value for the kingdom if Christians are drunk with ego, envy, or any form of evil. I've always wanted to be like the disciples at Pentecost, who seemed to be drunk but were filled with the Holy Spirit.

There is a trilogy of books called the *Hunger Games*. Some think the books are too centered "on kids killing kids." The stories are set in a future time when violence, human trafficking, totalitarianism, and evil are unchecked. But there is also sacrificial love, mercy, redemption, and hope. As Christians, we can often find the gospel even in secular books. Peeta Mellark is a baker's son who risks everything to help a starving girl. He is wounded and buries himself in the ground to hide. Three days later he emerges from a cave with new life and hope. We don't need a theological education to see this image of the resurrection of Jesus.

So now we return to resting our hope fully upon grace. Max Lucado, in his book called *Grace*, translates grace as "more than we deserve, greater than we can imagine." We can add that definition to the more traditional "unmerited love of God" toward us as sinners. Today, rest. Come to a complete STOP. Rest upon the hope that is brought to us by the revelation of Jesus Christ.

"Hope makes us better, not bitter." *–Anonymous*

~ 122 ~

1 Peter 1:21 (KJV) – *"Your faith and hope might be in God."*

Peter gives us an affirmation of faith. Translation for today: "Your trust and expectation of success will be in God." Affirm it again and again. Say it aloud. "My trust and hope (expectation of success) is in God." After writing some heavy theological teaching, Peter addresses "the pilgrims of the dispersion in Pontus, Galatia, Cappadocia, Asia, and Bithynia." He writes during their times of suffering and grief. It is one thing to evangelize and bring people to Christ; it is another to disciple them for confronting difficult times.

In our ministry at Ranch Hope, we have learned what Peter has learned. It is one challenge to have our young people accept Christ as their Savior; it is another to help prepare them for returning to a dysfunctional family or life in the "hood." The children we have been most successful with are those who have made a profession of faith and then moved on to Bible study or some form of Christian activity and shared their faith with others.

Mike was with us as a rebellious teenager. He had a terrible relationship with his mother, and she was glad to "put him" at Ranch Hope. Being fairly large for his age, he could be a handful. But there was a side to Mike that made him very likeable and popular with the other boys and staff. During the early

Dave Bailey

months at Ranch Hope he was influenced by his houseparents who helped him in his rehabilitation and redemption. We like to say our ministry is a place of R and R (rehabilitation and redemption). Mike completely changed—his relationship with his mother to his personal issues to his academic life and studies; even his athletic abilities improved. His faith and hope were now in God.

All of us confront difficult times in our walk with the Lord. This letter from Peter can be personalized for each of us. We have learned much from young people like Mike. Mike graduated from high school; he was an outstanding student and athlete. On the Ranch Hope campus he became a leader among his peers. After high school, he graduated from a college in Pennsylvania and then went on for a master's degree at a Christian college in Kentucky. Of course, each of these successes had their share of challenges. The Ranch stayed in touch with Mike and helped him keep his focus. He is now married with his own children and is helping other people, after being trained as a counselor. Of course, he has known many challenges since his time at Ranch Hope, but he has met them with his affirmation, "My faith and hope will be in God." Let's go and do likewise.

"When you come to the end of your rope, tie a knot and hold on." *–Franklin Delano Roosevelt*

~ **123** ~

1 Peter 3:15 – *"Share with others – the reason for the hope that we have with gentleness and respect."*

"Always share." I can still hear my mother's words. It was part of her early child training manual. (She was a student of Freud.) But we all knew there were times when some things were so good it was tough to share. (For me it was Mom's fried chicken or her coconut cake.) It was all for me!

It is also difficult for us to share or witness to our faith. We tend to think that Jesus' words, "Go ye into all the world and preach or teach the gospel" is reserved for evangelists or missionaries. Peter's message on hope gives us two important instructions: First, we are to share the reason for our hope. Of course, the reason for our hope is the Lord. All of our expectations of success are based on Him. As the familiar quote says, "Know Him, Know Hope—No Him, No Hope."

Second, we are not overbearing or callous in sharing the gospel, but rather gentle and respectful to the person we witness. Abrasive witnessing often turns off more people than it turns on.

As we read more of Peter's letter, we note that it is about the relationship of husband and wife, the relationship of Christian to Christian, and Christians suffering for righteousness' sake. Peter teaches that suffering can be a means to show our deep faith. How we respond to adversity can be a witness in itself. Even suffering caused by others who speak evil of us and falsely accuse us. Our hope is so strong and such a part of our daily routine that no form of suffering can take away our expectation of success.

Final Analysis

People are often unreasonable, illogical, and self-centered;
Forgive them anyway.
If you are kind, people may accuse you of selfish, ulterior motives;
Be kind anyway.
If you are successful, you will win some false friends and some true friends;
Succeed anyway.
If you are honest and frank, people may cheat you;
Be honest and frank anyway.
What you spend years building, someone could destroy overnight;
Build anyway.
If you find serenity and happiness, people may be jealous;
Be happy anyway.
The good you do today, people will often forget tomorrow;
Do good anyway.
Give the world your best witness anyway.

You see, in the final analysis, it is between you and God; it has never been between you and them anyway.

"A strong mind always hopes and always has cause to hope." *–Thomas Carlyle*

~ 124 ~

1 John 3:3 (NKJV) – *"Everyone who has this hope in Him purifies himself, just as He is pure."*

Interesting that the last verse on hope in the New Testament has to do with purity. That's right, purity—the act of being pure. We don't usually associate hope with purity, but the apostle John does, and it's a good subject to concentrate on as we conclude our study of hope. We have hope, and therefore we want to live a righteous and holy life.

Some historians have not been kind to the Puritans. Think of negative connotations of being puritanical—it is like a put-down. But it is good to remember the positive gifts of these early settlers to America. They had seen the spiritual depriva-tions of life in England —social and personal sins, alcoholism, poverty, sexual perversions, religious decay, political intrigue—and the Puritans wanted change. They wanted to "purify" an evil nation, and when they arrived on the American shore, it was their dream to start again, to find hope in a new land with the purity of the gospel.

Unfortunately, "holiness" is not on the top of the list for Christian preaching or teaching today. It is easy to find books and study guides about "self-improvement" or "motivation," but material on righteous living is difficult to obtain. Often derisive remarks like "holy Joe," "holier than thou," and "holy roller" say it all. But John has a different perspective.

John, in this letter, reminds us that hope leads us to a godly life. A person with hope will want to be clean, or as the detergent ad says, "Clean all over." As a child, my Saturday night bath was in a galvanized tub, with water heated on a coal stove in the kitchen. One bath a week, with sponge baths all week in the kitchen sink. You can image the dirt that weekly bath had to take off. But I came out of the tub feeling new all over. All of us in the family hoped for an indoor bathtub or shower. (At fifteen we moved to a home with indoor plumbing and a shower—what a blessing.) That's what hope can do for us today. Bathe in hope, feel clean all over, as the Lord purifies us to live a godly life.

William Longstaff wrote only one poem. He was a business man who gave to Christian causes and also wrote for Christian publications. After hearing a sermon "Be Ye Holy, for I Am Holy," he wrote down what holiness meant to him in the form of a poem. It was published in 1882 but soon forgotten until composer George Stebbins added music to the lyrics. We now sing:

> "Take this to be holy, speak oft with the Lord. Abide in him always, and feed on His word. Take time to be holy, the world rushes on; spend much time in secret with Jesus alone. By looking to Jesus, like Him thou shalt be; thy friends in thy conduct His likeness shall see."

This is holiness. Today, review the areas of your life where you have been cleaned up, and then commit to the Lord any areas of concern. Talk with God, and offer a sincere prayer for change.

> "Optimism is the faith that leads to achievement. Nothing can be done without hope and confidence."
> –Dale Carnegie

~ 125 ~

Proverbs 11:7 (NKJV) – *"When a wicked man dies, his expectation will perish, and the hope of the unjust perishes."*

A clean-cut warning for today: "Don't live a life separate from God and expect to have hope at death." It is very clear what Solomon is saying, and if any man had all this world has to give, it was Solomon. Speak of wealth, he had it. Speak of power, prestige, respect—all the amenities of wealth were Solomon's. But he knew they did not compute into hope.

Years ago Billy Graham made a statement in a sermon that has been oft quoted. It was used in a message about materialism and its negative effect upon the believer. Billy said, "Remember, you really cannot take it with you. I have never seen a U-Haul at the end of a hearse." Obviously, Billy Graham was making a serious statement in a humorous way! Relating this to today's Scripture, we can say "expectation of success at death will not be hooked on to the hearse."

Ke$ha is one of many strange and provocative entertainers today. A pop diva, she is the latest who has captured the attention of a generation of poisoned youth. My generation suffered through James Dean, Marlon Brando, Marilyn Monroe, and Elvis, just to name a few who lead the rebellion against parental and social authority. Now Ke$ha sings a song called "Die Young," which glorifies hard partying, lust, hedonism, and how life has no meaning. Solomon would have pulled the plug on this young woman's journey into nihilism. Jesus would have reminded her, "What does it profit a vocalist to gain the whole world and lose her soul (and take many youth with her)?"

Death is one statistic that never fails. For every human that is born, one dies. It is not a question of if, it is only a question of when and how. Many of the young people we have helped are all too familiar with death. A mother dies of a drug overdose, a father dies in a shootout in a bank, a brother or sister dies in a drive-by shooting, a grandparent succumbs to cancer. It is our goal to help young people find hope that does not perish and God's power that is eternal. Jesus also said, "I am the resurrection and the life. He that believes in me shall never die."

~ 126 ~

Proverbs 14:32 – *"Even in death the righteous have a hope."*

Like many proverbs, this is a lesson on contrast. It opens with the negative "the wicked are driven away in their wickedness, but (this is a BIG BUT) the righteous have hope even in facing death." Even in the greatest danger, the godly person will not lose their expectation of success. In the ministry, dealing with death is a common occurrence. Helping to counsel people facing death or reacting to the death of a loved one is a monumental work of grace. Hope must play a major role in people's coping with the "last enemy."

Obviously, this proverb was written a millennium before the resurrection of Jesus. What ancient Israel "hoped for," the Christian now knows as reality. The empty tomb gives the believer hope even in the face of death.

One of the key teachings of Proverbs is the fear of the Lord God (great respect), starting with verse 26. In this chapter, Solomon teaches that such fear brings confidence and a place of refuge (safety). Add to that imagery "the fear of the Lord is a fountain of life and it turns away the snares of death." All this leads you to the 32nd verse, which categorically states, "Even in death we have hope."

In Crozer Seminary I had a professor of Christian ethics, Dr. "Snuffy" Smith. (He had also taught Martin Luther King Jr., a graduate of Crozer). Dr. Smith told us of an experience he had with his four-year-old son. They were walking on the campus in Chester, Pennsylvania. The little boy noticed a tiny bird on the sidewalk that had fallen from the nest. Looking at the dead bird, he asked his father, "How come he had to die, Daddy?" Quite a question and quite a challenge for Dr. Smith, but he later told us that he said to the boy, "Honey, a bird can't fall from its nest without God knowing, and the Lord loved that little bird, too." I thought that was a great answer. I'm sure the little boy did not fully understand, as we don't when faced with death, but it helped at the time.

~ 127 ~

Lamentations 3:26 (KJV) – *"Hope and quietly wait for the salvation of the Lord."*

Lamentations is not a popular book of the Bible. In fact, I don't ever remember doing a series of sermons on this Old Testament book of poetry, nor hearing someone else do an exhaustive study of its message. In some ways the book is depressing, as the author deals with sorrow, pain, and misery. However, maybe that is why the word "hope" is so important to us to see against the backdrop of tragedy in "real life."

"Hope and quietly wait for the salvation of the Lord." Waiting is not one of our favorite exercises in life. How often have we heard the quote: "Make me patient, Lord, and hurry up!" But then we remember the scriptural message, "Those that wait upon the Lord shall renew their strength." Waiting is an important dimension of receiving the salvation of the Lord.

A few years ago, a Christian couple with their daughter, Erin, started a ministry called "Erin's Gift." The purpose of the ministry was to get teenagers and young adults involved in doing something worthwhile with their lives outside of the norm. For one week each summer they would go to areas and do construction, vacation Bible school, and athletic programs—whatever way their help was needed. It was hard work combined with lots of laughter and a big effort to make someone else's life a little better. Tragically, Erin was killed in a motor vehicle accident. Obviously, it was devastating to everyone. But the ministry continued; in fact, it grew. Everyone wanted to carry on this mission of hope. It is now called "Erin's Hope." My friends dealt with their sorrow, pain, and misery by waiting on the Lord. He has continued to bless them as a family and their outreach to help others.

The poet then ties in the word "quietly." Hope first, then wait, and do it quietly. Our culture does not put a lot of emphasis on quiet. Yet like the sign at the hospital, we all need a "quiet zone" in our spiritual life.

In the early months of Ranch Hope with our first twelve boys, my only "quiet" zone was late at night in an apartment. The boys were in bed (hopefully sleeping), and my own children were resting, as was Eileen. It was then after an exhaustive day that I had time to wait quietly for the continuing (my addition) salvation of the Lord. I encourage you to find hope today in your quiet zone.

> "God sees hope, where others see failure. God doesn't stop at ruins; it's where He begins." *–Ruth Graham*

~ 128 ~

Lamentations 3:29 (NKJV) – *"Let him put his mouth in the dust—There may yet be hope."*

Can you imagine your face in the dirt? Your mouth filled with dust? In ancient times, that was the sign of triumph for the aggressor. The vanquished (the loser) had his face in the dust, and the victor (the winner) had his foot on the loser's head, pushing down. This is another part of the imagery of a person "lamenting" how bad things are. But Jeremiah focuses on God, not the circumstances.

My good friend Charles Mandrake sent me an e-mail called, "Put It In God's Hands." It is worth sharing with you:

> A basketball in my hands is worth $27.00. In the hands of Michael Jordan, it was worth $33 million.
>
> A baseball in my hands is worth $6.00. In the hands of Alex Rodriquez, it is worth $57 million.

A football in my hands is worth $35.00. In the hands of Peyton Manning, it is worth $40 million.

A nail in my hands might produce a birdhouse. In the hands of Jesus, it produced salvation.

It's all according to in whose hands we put our hopes.

At this time I want you to perform a simple exercise that will illustrate this spiritual principle. Direct your attention to something in your room. For instance, focus on a piece of furniture, picture, or other item. Notice as you focus on that item that everything else in the room is out of focus (it is in your peripheral vision). We see most clearly what is in our focus, with everything else blurred.

For Jeremiah, it is time to focus on the promise of God and not the circumstances that surround us. To paraphrase Scripture, we could say that "where our focus is, there will our hearts be also." I had this proven to me in a very simple illustration. One year during our Methodist Camp Meeting, I decided to exercise with a ten-mile bike ride. All along the back roads and highway I saw trash carelessly discarded by people—everything from hamburger wrappers to beer cans. What a mess—litter, litter everywhere.

Upon returning to the camp, I told my wife about the disappointing experience. After listening sympathetically, she gave me some great advice: "Next time, focus on the beautiful woods, houses, and fields!" Great advice! A hope and its expectation of success remind me daily to focus on God's promises, not the devil's litter.

> "Lord, make me an instrument of thy peace; where there
> is hatred, let me sow love; where there is despair, hope."
> –*St. Francis of Assisi*

~ 129 ~

Psalm 119:74 (KJV) – *"They that fear thee will be glad when they see me; because I have hoped in thy word."*

In a recent publication that came to my home, this verse was included in an article that had the following literal translation: "They will see me and be glad." Hopeful people can help others be glad. People can see hope in us. And, of course, the psalmist wants us to remember that our hope comes from the Word of God. Will people be glad to see us?

Periodically on the Ranch Hope radio broadcast, I give an award to someone. We call it the Barnabas Award. You will remember that Barnabas was the encourager to the apostles and early Christians. He was born with the name Joseph, but because of his gift to encourage others, the Christian community nicknamed him Barnabas, Son of Encouragement. It was almost like calling him a cheerleader. Every family, every church, every ministry, every community needs a Barnabas. Maybe that could be your gift.

It is always interesting to listen to people and learn about their approach to life. I have said to someone, "My, it's a beautiful day," and their response was, "Yeah, but it's supposed to rain tomorrow." OK. Well, try again, Bailey. "You are really looking good." "I know, Dave, but I feel lousy inside." OK, try again, Bailey. "You have the greatest kids." "You think so, Dave? You ought to live with them." OK. Not much hope in that conversation, so it is my job to turn those negatives into positives. "Sunshine or rain, we have hope; feeling good or bad, we have hope; good kids or troubled kids, we have hope, and only because our life is centered in God's Word.

Don't miss that important point. The foundation of our hope comes from the Word. We have "hope in the Word." The psalmist wrote, long before Barnabas knew, that hope is based on the Word. We can surmise that Barnabas was into the Word (the Jewish Scriptures and not the gospel of Jesus). He was probably raised by godly parents that taught him the Law and the prophets. As we follow the story of Barnabas in the New Testament, we find that he did not have an easy life. At one time there was even a conflict with Paul. What makes his life so hopeful is that he continued to be an encourager. In an age when there is so much emphasis on being physically attractive, it should be our goal to be spiritually attractive. We want people to be glad when they see us and glad to be with us.

> "When I was young, my ambition was to be one of the people who made a difference in the world. My hope is to leave the world a little better for having been there."
> –*Jim Henson*

~ 130 ~

Psalm 119:116 (KJV) – *"And let me not be ashamed of my hope."*

Ashamed of hope? Seems incredible, but it is a grave concern of the psalmist at this point. He doesn't trust himself and pleads for God's help. This is a special moment when we can see the humanity of the writer and note a fear each of us must confront. It is one thing to be self-confident, but our real confidence must rest on the God who is beyond us. Stories are legion about political leaders, movie stars, even preachers, and others who are in the public arena that lose self-confidence. Their careers are almost destroyed and they must seek professional help to be restored. It is always a blessing to know of those who go through a spiritual transformation and turn to God in their need.

Years ago, my wife and I were sitting with our daughter, Lee Ann, in the Children's Hospital of Philadelphia. We became enraged by a mother and her attitude toward her severely handicapped child. We watched as the mother placed the child on a bench and then left him for a few moments. She came back and covered him with a blanket, with just a small area for his breathing. It soon became obvious that she was embarrassed to be associated with her impaired child. In one way or another, she was trying to disassociate herself from him in that waiting room. My wife and I both almost wept aloud. This woman was ashamed of her child.

Since that date, I have often prayed for that woman and child, hoping she has grown up and hoping the child has received the love and acceptance he needed. This story serves as an illustration to me of how I sometimes have been "ashamed of the gospel of Jesus Christ." In certain settings, under certain circumstances, I have almost tried to hide or neglect sharing the "hope that is within me." Our daughter that day also had severe impairments, but never once did we think of shielding her from other people. In fact, her personality was so vibrant, she attracted people. I have thought to myself, I want to be that way in terms of sharing Christ. Certainly, spiritually, I have some impairments, but I do not want to be ashamed of the gospel. Have you had a similar experience? There are times when we must accept our true humanity and cry out to God for help. "Let me not be ashamed of my hope."

"But what we call our despair is often only the painful ignorance of unfed hope." *–George Eliot*

~ 131 ~

Psalm 119:147 (KJV) – *"I prevented the dawning of the morning, and cried: I hoped in thy word."*

In the King James translation of the Bible, it is difficult to understand this verse because of the word "prevented." But, upon closer study, we find a marvelous message for today. A better translation would be, "Before the watchman proclaims the hour, I am awake, seeing God and meditating on His Word." Now we can begin to see the importance of this verse on hope. The NIV translation helps even more, "I rise before dawn and cry for help; I have put my hope in your word."

Historically, night for the Jews was divided into three watches of four hours each. The rotation started at six o'clock p.m. It was the Romans who instructed them to change this to four watches of three hours each. For this period of time each night, guards or watchmen would announce the end of one watch and the start of the next. It is not clear if the psalmist woke up at each announcement and prayed or if he prayed before the first watch at night and then the last one early in the morning. One or the other procedure was followed carefully and anchored him in hope.

Can you imagine being so excited about prayer and Bible study that you couldn't go to sleep? Now there have been all kinds of things that have kept me awake at night. Anxiety over a health condition, waiting news about a loved one who is in harm's way, restlessness as I listened for a child's coming home from a high school date, anticipating a challenge facing me the next day — all those can keep me awake, but again imagine being so focused on prayer and Bible study you stay awake. It is possible! What a blessing to fall asleep exhausted from talking to the Father and reading His Word. It will give us hope.

Robert Morgan wrote a small book on the importance of reading and even memorizing parts of the Bible. He writes, "Our minds are vaults especially designed to stockpile the seed of God's Word." He tells of a parishioner who was eighty-nine years old. She said memorizing Bible verses helped keep her mind fresh and young. What a way to beat the aging process!

For many years now I have started the day in meditation, Bible reading, and prayer. If I have a busy schedule for the day and must leave home early, it is imperative that I get up earlier and have more time alone with God. As has often been stated, "IF we are too busy for God, we're too busy." That is true for time alone in prayer and the Word. May I tell you candidly that I cannot give hope to troubled teenagers, or anyone else, until I am "prayed up" and "read up" myself. Have you discovered that truth?

"Losing hope, painful as it may seem, is the way to discover hope." *–David Augsburger*

~ 132 ~

Psalm 119:166 (KJV) – *"I have hoped for thy salvation, and done thy commandments."*

This entire section of this long psalm centers on the blessings that come from the Word of God. Our theme today highlights the word SALVATION. The author wants his readers to know that his hope is in the salvation of God. Because he has obeyed the commandments of God, there is no doubt in his mind that he has "expectations of success." Salvation is a key word in the Scriptures. Jesus came as our Savior. He came to seek and to save the lost. We are instructed by the word of God to "believe on the Lord Jesus and you will be saved." Little wonder that it has such a direct relationship to hope.

When I was in high school, a group of us from the youth group attended a conference for teenagers. The weekend was spent attending meetings dealing with concerns young people had and listening to speakers providing us with solutions. It was a time of fun, food, and fellowship. The climax of the conference was a speech by our bishop. Four hundred of us packed the auditorium to hear the bishop invite us to Christian service. I went forward. On the way home Sunday afternoon, a friend asked, "Why did you go forward, Dave?" Quick as a whip, I responded, "Because I'm gonna be a preacher!" His response startled me: "You can't be no preacher; you ain't been saved yet." My response was classic, "I don't have to be saved; I'm a Methodist." For me, salvation was going to church, being active in the choir, a leader of my youth group, and, of course, a Sunday school member. Needless to say, I have learned since that fateful afternoon as a teenager that Methodists also have to be saved. We, too, need to accept Christ as our personal Savior and build our life on hope in Him.

It took a number of years, however, for that statement from my friend to take root. He not only attended our local Methodist

Church, but his family was also involved with a Pentecostal Church. There was much more emphasis on "being saved" among the Pentecostals than at my local Methodist Church. It was not until college that I was confronted by a message from Billy Graham and later a challenge from a college roommate, George Douglas, and settled the question of being saved. There are many tracts that outline a plan that leads to the new life. I like this one:

The Roman Road to Salvation:

• For all have sinned, and come short of the glory of God (Romans 3:23).

• For the wages of sin is death (Romans 6:23a) but the gift of God is eternal life through Jesus Christ our Lord (Romans 6:23b).

• But God commended his love toward us, in that, while we were yet sinners, Christ died for us (Romans 5:8).

• For whosoever shall call upon the name of the Lord shall be saved (Romans 10:13).

• That if thou shalt confess with thy mouth the Lord Jesus, and shalt believe in thine heart that God hath raised him from the dead, thou shalt be saved (Romans 10:9).

Our greatest hope is to be on that road.

"My hope is built on nothing less than Jesus' blood and righteousness." –*Gospel hymn*

~ 133 ~

Proverbs 10:28 (NIV) – *"Hopes of the wicked come to nothing."*

If you read this passage in the King James Version, you will note it begins positively. "The hopes of the righteous shall be gladness; but the expectations of the wicked shall perish." Simply speaking, it means hope for the righteous will be realized, but that of the wicked will not. It is even more pronounced in the Living Bible: "The hopes of the wicked come to nothing." This particular series of proverbs can be traced directly to Solomon. Remember that Solomon spoke over three thousand proverbs and composed over one thousand songs. I have often wondered, did he have any ghost writers? Here in what we call the tenth chapter, he is offering contrasts, which we will often see in Proverbs. Today's contrast is between righteousness and wickedness. But this chapter begins by contrasting a wise son and a foolish son. It concludes by stating the difference between the mouth and lips of the righteous and unrighteous. Many contrasts are listed, one of which we now consider.

Not everyone's hope will be fulfilled. Expectations of success are based upon RIGHT LIVING. We cannot live like the devil and expect God to bless us with hope. How often I have learned this from former students. One in particular has gone from bad to worse. I always sympathize with his neglect as a child and the abuse he suffered, but I never let him use that as an excuse for negative behavior. His life has a sordid history—in and out of jail, in and out of relationships, in and out of debt and work, in and out of alcohol and drugs. He has had many opportunities to change. People have tried to help, a spiritual plan for his life has been offered and refused. Obviously, he has at times given us hope for his redemption and change. But these periods were short lived. His life has diminished hope for the future. Now he approaches the sixtieth year of his life very ill and alone.

Now my time to contrast. We called the young man "Pugs." I can still see him as a boy helping me clean the cottage and volunteer for other jobs that most of the kids avoided. At times it was difficult to believe he should even be at the Ranch, but a troubled home had taken its toll on his young life. He left the Ranch with positive goals and a relationship with the Lord. Over the years he worked hard, had a good marriage, raised great kids, and was well respected as an employee in his chosen vocation. Today he is retired and struggling with health issues, but his hope is not diminished. Two stories—contrasting lives — and we have seen the words of Solomon played out in real life.

Hopefully, today you and I can witness "the hope of the righteous shall be gladsome," or, as the New King James version reads, "The hope of the righteous will be gladness." Sing it with me: "He has made me glad, He has made me glad. I will rejoice for He has made me glad." Amen.

"Hope is the determination to keep us in the race when all seems lost." *–Roger Dawson*

A Final Thought

The Four Candles

Four candles slowly burned. The ambiance was so soft, one could almost hear them talking...

The first candle said: "I am Peace! The world is full of anger and fighting. Nobody can keep me lit." Then the flame of Peace went out completely.

The second candle said: "I am Faith! I am no longer indispensable. It doesn't make sense that I stay lit another moment." Just then a breeze softly blew out Faith's flame.

The third candle sadly began to speak: "I am Love! People don't understand my importance so they simply put me aside. They even forget to love those who are nearest to them." And waiting no longer, Love's flame went out.

Suddenly...a child entered the room and saw the three unlit candles. "Why aren't you burning? You're supposed to stay lit till the end." Saying this, the child began to cry.

Then the fourth candle answered: "Don't be afraid, I am Hope! While I am still burning we can relight the other candles."

With shining eyes, the child took the candle of Hope and relit the other candles.

The greatest of these is Love...but the flame of Hope should never go out of your life! With hope each of us can live with Peace, Faith, and Love.

Prayer

Dear God, You are my light and salvation. You are my hope. Please come into my heart, forgive all my wrongs, and give me Your wonderful gift of eternal Life. Help me be an instrument of Your love and cause Your light to shine on others through me. Amen.

To contact the author, email him at revbailey@ranchhope.org or send mail to P.O. Box 325, Alloway NJ 08001